GREATEST HIKES
IN CENTRAL COLORADO

SUMMIT AND EAGLE COUNTIES

A Hiking Guide

By Kim Fenske, JD, MST

Location of Hikes

TOPO! map printed on 05/28/06 from "GHikesTH.tpo"

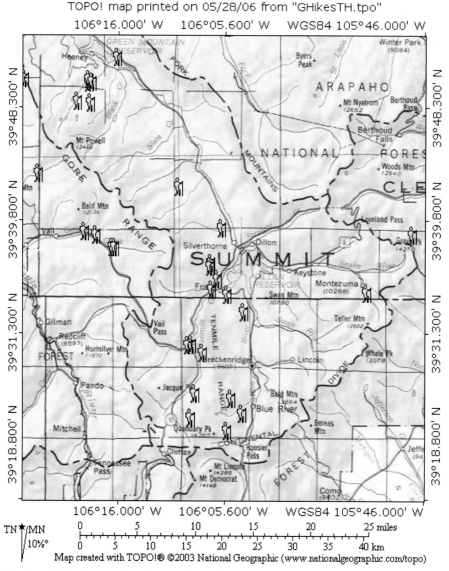

ISBN: 1-4276-0156-9

All maps within Greatest Hikes in Central Colorado are created using TOPO! ©2006 National Geographic on the internet at http://www.nationalgeographic.com/topo

Contents

Eagles Nest Wilderness Area

Continental Divide

Tenmile Range

Additional Features

Cataract Lake Loop Trail

Trailhead   39°50.224' N, 106°18.940' W
Destination   39°49.713' N, 106°19.643' W
Hours   1
Miles   2.3

The Eagles Nest and Ptarmigan Peak Wilderness Areas comprise 95,566 acres of primitive forest area within Summit County. The wilderness areas are a small part of the 2.3 million acres of the White River National Forest reserved for primitive recreation.

Wilderness designation for these areas means that natural forest conditions are protected by restricting motorized and wheeled vehicle traffic to areas outside the boundaries and limiting trail improvements to primarily native materials. A sense of isolation and solitude is maintained with group size limitations for recreation seekers and working livestock. Pets must be kept on leash to protect the safety and quietude of both wildlife and visitors.

Visitors are educated on "Leave No Trace" principles such as establishing dispersed campsites away from water sources, limiting campfire impact, and packing out trash. Although natural cycles of growth and destruction are normal to the forest, threats from invasive sources and human abuse pose challenges to the preservation of the biological communities in the wilderness.

Lower Cataract Lake looking east from the Eaglesmere Lakes Trail.

Eagles Nest Peak, namesake of Eagles Nest Wilderness Area.

Lower Cataract Lake rests at an elevation of about 8,600 feet. Eagles Nest Peak, elevation 13,342 feet, is the rock formation west of the lake that inspired the name of this wilderness area. The loop pathway begins across Cataract Creek at the eastern shoreline of Lower Cataract Lake. Southeast of Lower Cataract Lake, the Williams Fork Range can be viewed across Green Mountain Reservoir and the Blue River.

The area surrounding Lower Cataract Lake is a transition from high desert to an alpine environment. Therefore, visitors can enjoy a range of communities from open views of sagebrush fields, aspen, *Populus tremuloides*, in meadows coated with the colors of wildflowers, and nearly-impenetrable conifer forests of lodgepole pine, *Pinus contorta*, spruce, and fir.

Within the Lower Cataract Lake area, visitors can find a wide variety of wildflowers from the middle of June, when snowdrifts are still receding, to the middle of August. Expect daytime high temperatures to reach 80 degrees during the day and 40 degrees at night.

Blue bonnet,
Lupinus bakeri bakeri.

Cinquefoil,
Potentilla pulcherrima.

Sunflower,
Genus Helianthus.

Wild rose,
Rosa woodsii.

Lupines, a variety of blue-colored species among the *Lupinus* genus, line the shoreline of Lower Cataract Lake and are one of the first wildflowers encountered. The invasive weed oxeye daisy, *Leucanthemum vulgare,* was introduced to the grassy meadows near the east side of Lower Cataract Lake.

Cinquefoil is a common yellow flower in the area. Asters, in the *Asteraceae* or sunflower family, also enjoy sharing the fields above Lower Cataract Lake with the aspen. Along the shoreline, both the sunflower and wild rose bask in breaks among the trees.

At the first left fork in the trail, the wild geranium, *Geranium caespitosum*, opens lavender-lobed blossoms in the meadow. False forget-me-not, *Hackelia floribunda*, grows to waist height along the south and north sides of Lower Cataract Lake, with showers of pale blue clusters covering the slopes. Peavine, *Lathyrus leucanthus*, shows several color variations from purple to white throughout the watershed. Cow parsnip, *Heracleum spondylium*, grows in wetlands of the area.

Turning left at the second junction in the trail presents the flower-filled higher meadows at the south end of Lower Cataract Lake. Green gentian, *Fraseria speciosa*, dominates the upper meadows, rising to a height of six feet with white cross blossoms. Unsurprisingly, green gentian is also known as monument plant. Paintbrush grows in several color variations throughout the Gore Range, including yellow, pink, and red. Paintbrush, genus *Castilleja*, is hemiparasitic, dependent on nutrients from the roots of other plants within its community.

Wild geranium,
Geranium caespitosum.

False forget-me-not,
Hackelia floribunda.

Purple peavine,
Lathyrus leucanthus.

Cow parsnip,
Heracleum spondylium.

The fairy trumpet, *Gilia aggregata,* blazes scarlet petals among the prairie grasses on slopes overlooking the south shore of Lower Cataract Lake. The distinctive foot-high stem holds brilliant five-point trumpets along its stem filled with nectar to attract local hummingbirds.

Columbine covers the fertile meadows at the south end of Lower Cataract Lake, a third of a mile along the south shore of Lower Cataract Lake Loop. The magnificent blue columbine, *Aquilegia caerulea*, is the state flower of Colorado. Columbine is named after the Latin for dove, *columba*, for its delicate winged petals that often hover over pools of water.

Many native representatives of the Aster family also greet hikers on the trails throughout Summit County. A cluster of yellow subalpine arnica glow brightly beside a large fallen spruce log at a turn before the mouth of Cataract Creek. One mile along the Lower Cataract Lake Loop, a bridge crosses the tumbling waters of Cataract Creek. Beside the bridge, bunchberry dogwood, *Cornus canadensis,* blooms with white flowers set against dark green leaves in the damp and sheltered ground.

Beyond Cataract Creek at the west end of the lake is a wetland meadow of deep muck soil covered in shoulder-high leaves of cornhusk lily, *Veratrum tenuipetalum*, topped with small white flowers. In shaded areas of fertile soil along the shore beyond the field of cornhusk lily, the dark purple lobes of monkshood dwell. A poisonous plant, monkshood sap was used by early hunters to poison arrowheads. *Aconitum dephinifolium*, is also known as wolfbane, a member of the buttercup family.

Green gentian,
Fraseria speciosa.

White peavine,
Lathyrus leucanthus.

Yellow paintbrush,
Genus Castilleja.

Oxeye daisy, an invasive weed,
Chrysanthemum leucanthemum..

Blue columbine,
Aquilegia coerulea.

One-headed daisy,
Erigeron simplex.

Subalpine arnica,
Arnica mollis.

Bunchberry dogwood,
Cornus canadensis.

A patch of nettle-leaved giant hyssop, *Agastache urticifolia*, a mint, tumbles across the trail to the lake at the north end of the wetland meadow. On higher ground at the north end of Lower Cataract Lake, near the cliff overlook of uplifted rock, the mariposa lily, *Calochortus gunnisonii*, blooms.

In the upland meadows, beardtongue, *Penstemon hallii*, yawns open its large tubular blooms, joined by other blue penstemons and chiming bells of the family *Boraginaceae*. Fireweed from the primrose family also fills the fields with colorful blossoms.

Cornhusk lily,
Veratrum tenuipetalum.

Monkshood,
Aconitum columbianum.

Nettle-leaved giant hyssop,
Mentha Agastache urticifolia.

Mariposa lily,
Calochortus gunnisonii.

Beardtongue,
Penstemon halli halli.

Fireweed,
Genus *Chamerion.*

For more information:

Topographic Maps

Green Mountain Reservoir, Ute Pass, #107, National Geographic Maps, P.O. Box 4357, Evergreen, CO 80437-4357, 800-962-1643, 303-670-3457, www. nationalgeographic.com/maps.

Wildflowers

Guide to Colorado Wildflowers, G. K. Guennel, Westcliffe Publishers, Inc., P.O. Box 1261, Englewood, CO 80150, www.westcliffepublishers.com.

Noxious Weeds

Colorado Department of Agriculture Noxious Weed Program, 700 Kipling Street, Suite 4000, Lakewood, CO 80215-8000, 303-239-4182, eric.lane@ ag.state.co.us.

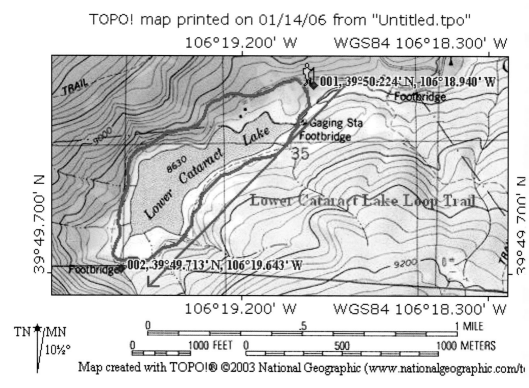

TOPO! map printed on 01/14/06 from "Untitled.tpo"

Map created with TOPO! ©2006 National Geographic
http://www.nationalgeographic.com/topo

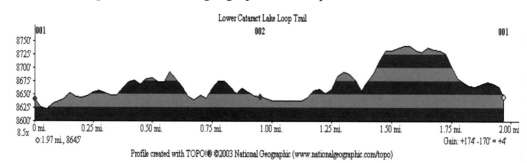

Profile created with TOPO!® ©2003 National Geographic (www.nationalgeographic.com/topo)

The Cataract Lake Loop Trail starts at 8,650 feet and rises along the north shore to 8,770 feet for 120 feet of elevation gain.

Sawatch Range of Holy Cross Wilderness Area southwest of Elliot Ridge.

Elliot Ridge Trail

Trailhead	39°50.489' N, 106°25.372' W
Destination	39°45.468' N, 106°22.275' W
Hours	6
Miles	11

Access to the Eagles Nest Wilderness Area often means hiking uphill for several thousand feet over steep terrain. One exception to the rule of scrambling up steep slopes to reach the tree line is the entry along Spring Creek Ranch Road that leads to Elliot Ridge Trail. Forest Service roads branching near the northern boundary of the Eagles Nest Wilderness Area in Grand County allow access by high clearance vehicles to the heights of the Gore Range.

In the fall, the drive up Spring Creek Ranch Road offers switchbacks overlooking colorful aspen groves. Hunters frequent the elk management area west of the Lower Blue River below Green Mountain Reservoir because of the meadow breaks created by forest management practices in this area. The Forest Service roads above Spring Creek Ranch Road are open to off-highway vehicle recreation up to the wilderness boundary.

The rugged Gore Range peaks provide a sharp line of delineation between Summit and Eagle Counties. The Elliot Ridge Trail slices the spine of the Gore Range and offers expansive views east to the Ptarmigan Wilderness Area and southwest to the Holy Cross Wilderness Area. Since most of the trail is above the tree line, avoid hiking in the area during thunderstorms.

The hike from the junction at the Blue Lake parking area to Meridian Peak and back is 15 miles in length, with an elevation change from 11,170 feet to 12,630 feet. At an average moving speed of 2 miles an hour, the entire hike takes 8 hours. The drive from Silverthorne is 39 miles to the trailhead, adding another hour to the adventure.

In order to reach the trailhead, drive north from Silverthorne on Highway 9 to Mile Marker 128, passing Williams Peak Road on the right. Turn west on Spring Creek Ranch Road, Grand County 10, and drive up 6 miles to the White River Forest snowmobile winter access parking area. Continue upslope along Forest Service Road 1831, marked with orange diamonds, to reach the Blue Lake junction, 12.7 miles from Highway 9, at 39°50.489' N, 106°25.372' W. Beginning at about 11.5 miles, several high-clearance water diversions require cautious driving. The final descent to the Elliot Ridge Trailhead is deeply rutted and may be muddy. Parking along the forest access road above Blue Lake is prudent. As a point of reference, the descent 3 miles on the next spur of road leads to the Gore Range Trailhead at Mahan Lake.

Meridian Peak, 12,630 feet, with sheer drops of 2,000 feet from the trail.

Collared pika, *Ochotona collaris.*

After passing the little pond on the left referred to as Blue Lake, a registration station marks the trail among a field of boulders. Red elderberry, *Sambucus microbotrys*, marks the entrance to the trail. Then, the trail turns briefly to the west past Sheephorn Mountain and passes patches of red prickly currant, *Grossulariacere Ribes montigenum*. Respect the wilderness beyond the trail signs by leaving no trace of visitation.

Rising to the ridge, the trail ascends more than a thousand feet over gracefully undulating alpine meadows. Looking eastward, Green Mountain appears directly perpendicular to the trail. After two hours, Mirror Lake Trail crosses a saddle in the ridge, allowing a descent to Mirror, Upper Cataract, Cat, and Surprise lakes. However, another hour of gentle ascent to the South leads to the first summit at 12,400 feet. Continuing along a craggy ridge, on a trail suited to a mountain goat, leads to Meridian Peak at a summit of 12,630 feet, 39°45.468' N, 106°22.275' W.

For More Information:

Virtual Dillon Ranger District, Elliot Ridge Trail map and description, http://dillonrangerdistrict.com/summer/ellrid_hkg.htm

Red elderberry, *Sambucus microbotrys.*

Red prickly currant, *Grossulariacere Ribes montigenum.*

Mountain goat, *Oreamnos americanus.*

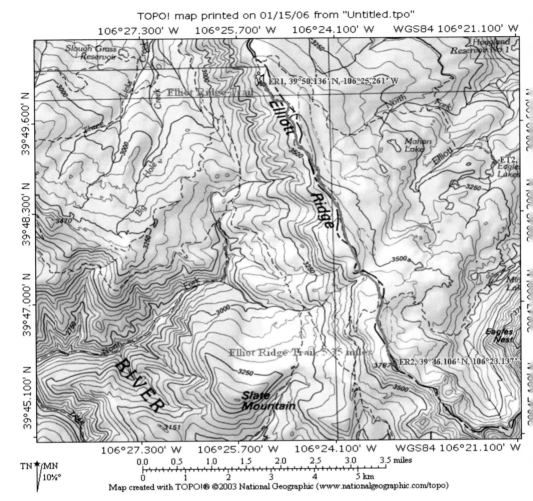

Map created with TOPO! ©2006 National Geographic
http://www.nationalgeographic.com/topo

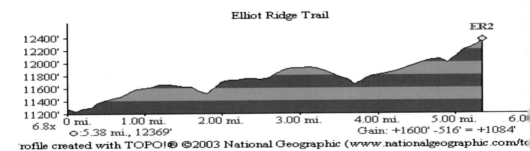

The Elliot Ridge Trail starts at 11,170 feet and rises to 12,630
feet along a gently rising slope for 1,460 feet of elevation gain.

The Williams Fork Range lies east of the Eagles Nest Wilderness Area.

Eaglesmere Lakes Trail

Trailhead   39°50.391' N, 106°18.823' W
Destination   39°48.992' N, 106°21.451' W
Hours   5
Miles   7

The Eagles Nest and Ptarmigan Peak Wilderness Areas comprise 95,566 acres of primitive forest area within Summit County. The wilderness covers most of the Gore and Williams Fork Ranges from Silverthorne, Frisco, and Copper Mountain in the South to Heeney along the Green Mountain Reservoir in the North. The wilderness areas are magnificent areas to explore, respect, and admire. Although natural cycles of growth and destruction are normal to the forest, threats from invasive sources and human abuse also pose challenges to the preservation of the biological communities in the wilderness.

Healthy lodgepole pine is dense and lush green.

Entry by mountain pine beetles are marked by sap defenses.

Lodgepole pine after attack by mountain pine beetle larvae.

Parasitic mistletoe eventually kills lodgepole pine trees.

A great location for spring wilderness adventure is the Eaglesmere Lakes Trail. Located 24 miles north of Silverthorne, the trail wanders through the north end of the Gore Range.

Eaglesmere Lakes Trail ascends from an elevation of about 8,700 feet to 10,400 feet. The path has a southern exposure during its gradual ascent to provide great views of the Eagles Nest Peak, elevation 13,342 feet, the rock formation that inspired the name of this wilderness area. From open out-croppings in aspen meadows, the Eaglesmere Lakes Trail also affords views of Lower Cataract Lake, Green Mountain Reservoir, and the Williams Fork Range.

Approach the Eaglesmere Lakes Trail by driving north on Highway 9 from Silverthorne. At the 118 mile marker, turn left along the road to Heeney and wind 5 miles along the west shore of Green Mountain Reservoir. After pass-ing the developed campgrounds of Davis Springs, Prairie Point, and McDon-ald Flats, turn west and travel 2 miles up Cataract Creek Road, a gravel road through upland desert sagebrush.

Above Cataract Campground, there are three trailheads. Bear right to the Eaglesmere Lakes Trailhead, straight for Lower Cataract Lake Trailhead, and use the parking area along the road to the left for the Surprise Lake Trail-head. The area is part of a Forest Service Fee Demonstration Area, so there is a required daily or annual pass available to raise funds to help maintain the trails.

Serviceberry,
Amelanchier alnifolia.

Orange agoseris,
Agoseris aurantiaca.

****

Valid For
15% OFF
One regularly priced item
on your next purchase*

CALL 1-800-669-4037

Please call within 2 days.
Take an easy survey about your most
recent experience at this Borders.

When prompted, enter the following
code:
0545-0725-0601-3385

Write in the 8-digit coupon code
provided at the end of the survey

1530011000

*Some restrictions may apply
*Expiration date: 90 days from date of
original receipt

POS: S1, S5, coupon A, 15%

0545   REG: 13, 4   KR: 382
       07/26/2008   TR: 0061

****

Musk thistle,
Carduus nutans macrolepis.

White thistle,
Cirsium canescens.

Casual observation of the meadows surrounding Lower Cataract Lake in mid-summer reveals infestation by the white flowers of false chamomile, *Matricaria maritima*, and oxeye daisy, *Chrysanthemum leucanthemum.* Other invasive plant species in the area include musk thistle, *Carduus nutans macrolepis,* mullein,*Verbascum thapsus,* curly dock, *Rumex triangulivalvis,* and yellow toadflax, *Linaria vulgaris.*

An initiative by the Friends of the Eagles Nest Wilderness in cooperation with the Forest Service developed an inventory and treated areas of the wilderness and adjacent fields where these pests are spreading. Visitors interested in assisting with projects to protect the wilderness biodiversity are urged to apply to the Volunteer Wilderness Steward Program.

From the trailhead parking area, the Eaglesmere Lakes Trail climbs westward along a shallow ravine through groves of aspen. In spring, flocks of purple finches dine on seeds among the aspen. Grouse sun themselves on the rocky outcroppings along the trail. Signs of elk, mule deer, and bear are abundant in the melting snow, with chew marks cut into the bark of many aspen from winter foraging.

Within an hour of climbing up the trail, Lower Cataract Lake can be seen in the valley below the aspen. Looking to the southeast, the Williams Fork range can be observed in the Ptarmigan Peak Wilderness. Across the valley is the dense lodgepole pine forest that hides Surprise, Cat, Upper Cataract, Mirror, Tipperary, and Eaglesmere Lakes within the Cataract Creek watershed.

As the trail rises into the midst of the lodgepole pine, *Pinus contorta*, watch for trees that are bleeding sap, the entry wounds of the mountain pine beetle, *Dendroctonus ponderosae*, an insect pest that is killing significant swathes of lodgepole pine throughout Summit County. Each year, the mountain pine beetle mates and produces close to a hundred offspring per pair. The beetles commonly reach the adult stage by late July and may expand an area of infestation by tenfold. Small round holes in the lodgepole bark are the exit wounds created by the exit of adult mountain pine beetles.

Infestation of the forest by insects is part of the natural cycle of death and re-birth in the forest. The insect population growth helps stimulate predation by woodpeckers, which may kill more than half of the adult beetles by removing the bark an infested tree. Below-zero temperatures over extended periods of winter also lead to very high mortality for bark beetle populations, stemming epidemics. However, drought and abnormally warm winters have aided the mountain pine beetle to rapidly spread throughout Summit County in recent years.

Another deadly pest that is common among dense stands of lodgepole pine is dwarf mistletoe, *Arceuthobium americanum*. Dwarf mistletoe is a parasite that shoots seeds through the air to infect nearby trees with yellow growths that often engulf the needles of the conifer. Over several years, the pine tree may develop swollen branches or exhibit twisted multiple-branch develop-ment called witches' brooms.

Chamomile,
Matricaria maritima.

Mullein,
Verbascum thapsus.

Curly dock,
Rumex triangulivalvis.

Yellow toadflax,
Linaria vulgaris.

Soft pine tree species like the lodgepole and jack pine are susceptible to attack by dwarf mistletoe. Therefore, one way to ensure healthy stands of forest is intermingling spruce, fir, and aspen among the lodgepole pine and thinning infected stands to prevent the transmission of mistletoe to healthy trees.

Approximately 3 miles from the trailhead, the Eaglesmere Lakes Trail meets the Gore Range Trail. Bearing to the right leads to the two Eaglesmere Lakes after a half-mile climb with 200 feet of elevation gain. Across the lakes to the south, the Eagles Nest looms above the forest. Boulder mazes along the north shore of the lakes provide a resting place for dining and contemplation.

If Eaglesmere Lakes are a morning destination, the afternoon can be spent circling the valley. Returning south along the Gore Range Trail extends the hike past Tipperary Lake and, eventually, leads to Surprise Lake. From Surprise Lake, the descent should take about an hour to the trailhead east of Lower Cataract Lake.

For More Information:

Virtual Dillon Ranger District, Eaglesmere Lakes Trail map and description, http://dillonrangerdistrict.com/summer/eaglak_hkg.htm

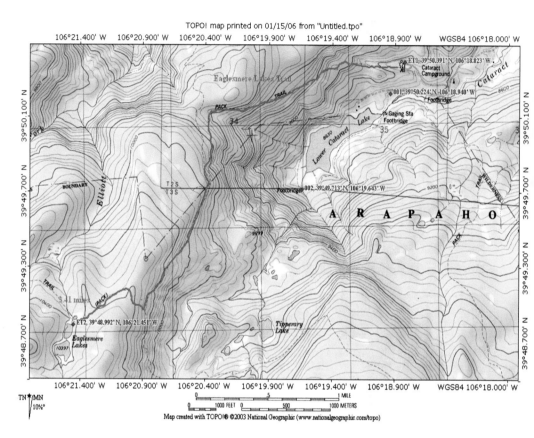

Map created with TOPO! ©2006 National Geographic
http://www.nationalgeographic.com/topo

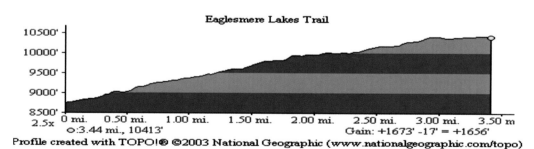

The Elaglesmere Lakes Trail starts at 8,700 feet to 10,400 feet
along a moderate slope for 1,700 feet of elevation gain.

Green Mountain lies north of Cow Creek Campground.

Green Mountain Reservoir Trail

Trailhead	39°52.769' N, 106°16.665' W
Destination	39°52.643' N, 106°17.134' W
Hours	1
Miles	1

Green Mountain Reservoir is a largely unappreciated natural resource of Summit County. In spring, the high desert that surrounds the reservoir is lushly carpeted in wildflower blooms. During the summer, Green Mountain Reservoir provides spacious boating, fishing, hiking, biking, off-road vehicle, and car camping recreational opportunities.

Green Mountain Reservoir contributes to the Front Range water supply by means of the Colorado-Big Thompson Project. The dam project began in 1938 and contributes 21 megawatts of renewable electricity to Colorado.

When full, Green Mountain Reservoir has a surface area of approximately 2,125 acres. The lake elevation in spring is about 7,900 feet, with peak elevation at 7,950 feet in summer. Wind-surfing, water-skiing, swimming, kayaking, diving, and other water activities are permitted in the reservoir.

Power boat access points include a ramp at Cow Creek South Campground, another between Willows and the dam at the north end of the lake, and Mc-Donald Flats Campground.

The existing Forest Service campgrounds around Green Mountain Reservoir are Davis Springs, Prairie Point, McDonald Flats, Elliott Creek, Willows, Cow Creek North, and Cow Creek South. In addition, there is a remote camp-ground up Cataract Creek that primarily serves as a gateway for backpack-ing trips into the Eagles Nest Wilderness Area. The entire area is classified as a Recreation Enhancement Area, which requires the payment of self-ser-vice fees and placement of a receipt in each vehicle windshield for day use as well as overnight stays.

Most of the campgrounds do not provide potable water, so campers should pack large containers of drinking water or bring a water filtration system. Modern, odorless, handicap-accessible pit toilets were recently constructed to serve the Cow Creek area. The Forest Service provides metal fire rings for use in developed campsite loops along the dirt roadways within the campgrounds.

Construction of rock ring campfires and waste disposal on the beaches are not permitted for public safety and environmental health reasons. Carry fire containment gear such as a grill, trash bags to gather litter, and a camper toilet for dispersed beach camping. Please respect posted regulations.

Green Mountain projects skyward at the north end of the lake and offers climbing opportunities. Below the peak, the surrounding hills are high desert, covered in sagebrush. In the sagebrush, wildflowers bloom.

Rock rings and trash create public safety hazards near the reservoir.

Members of the buttercup family, *Ranunculus*, reflect the sun with their rounded, golden blooms. The mountain ball cactus, *Pediocactus simpsonii*, swells renewed with spring rains to erupt in shades of pink and cream. Bundles of moss campion, *Silene acaulis subacaulenscens*, sprout points of five-petal pink stars like cluster bombs across the sand. White petals burst from the green carpet woven by the alpine phlox, *Phlox condensata*.

Like bleeding elk antlers, spikes of Wyoming paintbrush, stick brilliant scarlet probes with yellow veins out from beneath branches of sagebrush. In the moist meadows, Chiming bells, *Mertensia virdis*, droop bunches of grape florets that drip in sugar for arriving hummingbirds.

The high desert blooms of Green Mountain Reservoir can be found 24 miles north of Silverthorne along Colorado State Highway 9. A few miles past the southern junction with Heeney Road, look for the Forest Service signs for Prairie Point, Cow Creek South, Cow Creek North. Take a left turn to Willows at the northern intersection with Heeney Road and the boat ramp before the dam. After the dam, along the southwest side of the reservoir, wander past Elliot Creek, Heeney, Cataract Creek Road, McDonald Flats, and Davis Springs.

For Further Information:

Dillon Ranger District, 680 River Parkway, P.O. Box 620, Silverthorne, CO, 80498, Phone: 970-468-5400

Bureau of Reclamation, http://www.usbr.gov/gp-bin/arcweb_gmtr.pl

Mountain ball cactus, *Pediocactus simpsonii*.

Mountain ball cactus blooms at Green Mountain Reservoir.

Mountain bluebell,
Mertensia virdis.

Wyoming paintbrush,
Castilleja linariaefolia.

Moss campion, *Silene acaulis
subacaulenscens.*

Alpine phlox,
Phlox condensata.

TOPO! map printed on 01/15/06 from "Colorado.tpo"

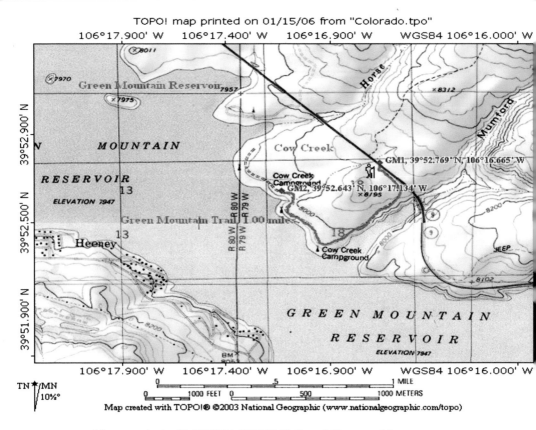

Map created with TOPO! ©2006 National Geographic
http://www.nationalgeographic.com/topo

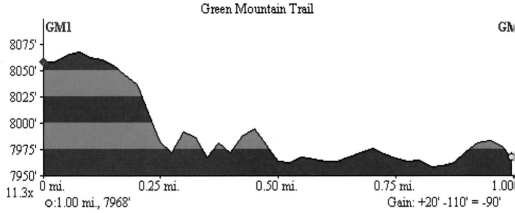

Green Mountain Trail

Green Mountain Reservoir Trail at Cow Creek Campground
begins at an elevation of 8,050 feet and descends to 7,950 feet.

Wetlands above Mirror Lake rest within an amphitheater of mountains.

Mirror Lake Trail

Trailhead	39°50.17' N, 106°18.659' W
Destination	39°47.432' N, 106°21.326' W
Hours	10
Miles	13

The north end of the Gore Range provides access to dramatic rock outcroppings, plunging streams filled with prolific trout, and alpine lakes at the base of sheer amphitheaters created by summits exceeding 13,000 feet in height. Winding through the valley of Cataract Creek is the westward ascending Mirror Lake Trail. The 6.5 mile climb to Mirror Lake takes about 5 hours, with Elliot Ridge and Meridian Peak, 12,390 feet, accessible on the trail beyond within another few hours.

The Mirror Lake Trail is an offshoot of the Surprise Lake Trail at the north end of the Eagles Nest Wilderness Area. Surprise Lake Trailhead is 25 miles north of Silverthorne. Take Highway 9 to the 118 mile marker and turn west on Heeney Road, Summit County Road 30. After 5.3 miles, turn west and climb along Cataract Creek Road, a narrow gravel surface.

Pass Cataract Creek Campground, hidden among the spruce and aspen along the edge of a high desert sage meadow, on the left side of the road. Immediately past the campground is a junction, with a left fork to the Eagles-mere Trailhead. A few hundred feet ahead is the parking area and fee collection station for Surprise Trailhead to Mirror Lake.

The Surprise Lake Trail, 39°50.17' N, 106°18.659' W, begins at 8,597 feet, ascending 2.6 miles to 10,085 feet. Cross the bridge over Cataract Creek, then climb through a sage meadow into the Eagles Nest Wilderness Area. During the first hour of the climb, hike across the rich soil of several aspen meadows filled with blue Colorado columbine, Aquilegia coerulea, scarlet fairy trumpet, Gilia aggregata, and alpine yarrow, Achillea alpicola. Among the spruce and fir along the path, a large gray beetle with white spots, the Oregon fir sawyer, Monochamus oregonensis, resides among the evergreens.

Fleeting distant sightings of bears, coyotes, and mountain lions are common along the lower section of trail near the Cataract Creek. Yellow-bellied marmots dig deep burrows into the rock strewn sage meadow across from the trailhead. Dogs must be restrained with a leash to protect wildlife and as a courtesy to hikers frequenting the area.

After the meadows and a wide stream crossing, the trail begins a steeper ascent through a dense lodgepole forest. Notice the water diversions made of rock and water checking steps constructed by Forest Service trail crews and Friends of the Eagles Nest Wilderness volunteers. These structures attempt to shed running water from the central tread of the trail and reduce the force of water eroding a deep channel into the mountain slope.

Mirror Lake is nestled among rugged peaks near tree-line.	Cataract Creek flows from Meridian Peak.

On more level terrain closer to Surprise Lake, cuts into the sides of the trail drain puddles to keep the center tread dry. The diversions make hiking during summer storms less messy and minimize braiding of the trail by hikers who trample the edges to avoid getting muddy. The lower branches of spruce trees and lodgepole pines that interfered with horse and hiker traffic are pruned back to prevent widening of the trail. Since 20 percent of any mature forest is dead, trees that fall across the trail are also removed to ease travel and eliminate detour trails that compact soil and destroy the plants in the forest understory.

After 1.5 hours of climbing, watch for an area of concentrated dead falls removed with a cross cut saw. The Surprise Lake Trail joins the Gore Range Trail near a tumble of downed trees. Turning left, the Gore Range Trail turns east and descends to Otter Creek and passes through private grazing lands along Black Creek. Take the right fork on the Gore Range Trail, heading west, and climb the last 15 minutes to Surprise Lake.

A few large logs form a crossing of the brook that descends from the spongy wetland along the northern shore of Surprise Lake. The woodland along the western shore of the lake is a good example of densely compacted soil, void of plant life from years of heavy use and occupation by campers.

Ascend west for another 30 minutes along the Gore Range Trail to the junction with the Upper Cataract Lake and Mirror Lake Trail. Sit on the large diameter log that I cut from the trail and rolled down to the junction to create a rest area. The junction is a great location to drink water and eat lunch before proceeding to the upper lakes.

Mountain goldenrod, *Solidago multiradiata scopulorum.*

Mountain gentian, *pneumonanthe parryi.*

The next segment of the hike is about 1 hour to Upper Cataract Lake. About mid-way to Upper Cataract Lake is a boggy area lined with many wetland flower blossoms including purple monkshood, Aconitum columbianum, mountain goldenrod, Solidago mutiradiata, and mountain gentian, Pneumonaenthe parryi.

As you break out of the forest overlooking a boulder field, Cat Lake, 10,600 feet, glistens in the afternoon sun a few hundred feet below Upper Cataract Lake. Descend along a winding path across the rock and cross a stream lined with the blooms of white marsh marigold, Psychrophia leptosepala, in early summer. Upper Cataract Lake, 10,744, is uphill from the trail. The Eagles Nest, 13,397, towers above the steep rock face across the lake.

The trail rises to about 11,000 feet, where you can pause to view the Cataract Creek valley and Elliot Ridge from the cliffs at the edge of the trail. Rock switchbacks descend to a crossing of Cataract Creek. Immediately across the creek, observe a confusing labyrinth of social trails descending to the right. In the dark, you can easily miss the stream crossing because of these social trails. If you have any doubts about finding the crossing, throw down the limb of a dead tree to block the descending path and point toward Cataract Creek for the return ascent along the valley wall. Remember to reserve enough energy to ascend to Upper Cataract Lake on the return trip.

Turning southwest, ascend beside the tumbling cataracts that lead almost immediately to the north shoreline of Mirror Lake, 39°47.432' N, 106°21.326' W, 10,560 feet. Proceeding beyond Mirror Lake, you can hike across open wetlands surrounded by an amphitheater formed by Meridian Peak, 12,390 feet, to the west. The Mirror Lake Trail ascends for nearly 2,000 feet to Elliot Ridge, offering an entire day of hiking in the tundra above tree-line.

Oregon fir sawyer, *Monochamus oregonesis*, feeds on evergreen trees.

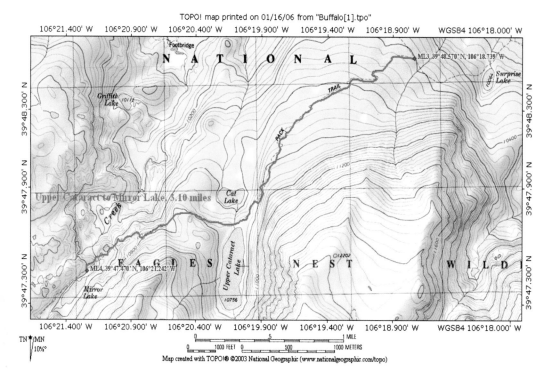

TOPO! map printed on 01/16/06 from "Buffalo[1].tpo"

Map created with TOPO! ©2006 National Geographic
http://www.nationalgeographic.com/topo

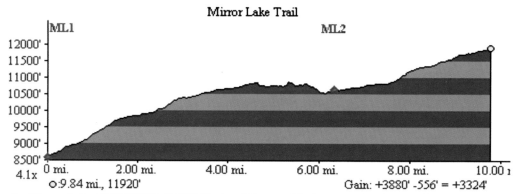

Mirror Lake Trail begins at an elevation of 8,600 feet and
ascends to 10,560 feet.

Tipperary Lake rests peacefully beneath the Eagles Nest.

Tipperary Lake Trail

Trailhead   39°50.364' N, 106°18.827' W
Destination   39°48.895' N, 106°19.939' W
Hours   6
Miles   9

The Gore Range Trail extends 43 miles from its southern end at Copper Mountain to Mahan Lake at the northern entrance to the Eagles Nest Wilderness Area. An easy access point, with a loop for day hikers, begins at the Eaglesmere Lakes Trailhead, 39°50.364' N, 106°18.827' W, and ends at Surprise Trailhead, 39°50.171' N, 106°18.659' W, near Lower Cataract Lake. The entire loop takes about six hours for a day hiker, with a starting elevation of 8,700 feet rising to 10,250 feet.

Eaglesmere Lakes Trailhead is approximately 24 miles north of Silverthorne. Take Highway 9 north to the 118 mile marker, then turn left onto Heeney Road and drive four miles along the west side of the Blue River and Green Mountain Reservoir. Turn left again at Cataract Creek Road, drive two miles up the gravel road to Cataract Creek Campground. Take the right branch at the next junction of the road for Eaglesmere Trailhead.

Proceed up the Eaglesmere Trail along the north side of the valley on a gradual ascent through aspen meadows to reach a junction with the Gore Range Trail. Along the way, the high desert slopes are covered in sage and service berry, then transition to aspen meadows filled in summer with Aspen daisies, *Erigeron speciosa*, fireweed, *Chamerion augustifolium*, and harebell, *Campanula rotundifolia*. Northern bedstraw, *Galium septentrionale*, imported by northern Europeans to fill mattress ticks, hides in the shaded woodland beside brooks that cross the trail. Red columbine, *Aquilegia elegantula*, is among the first of the native wildflowers to cover these slopes among the aspen in spring.

The Gore Range Trail is two and a half hours uphill at an elevation of about 10,250 feet. Hike south along the Gore Range Trail. The trail crosses a wetland where spotted coralroot, *Corallorhiza maculata*, digests fallen trees and subalpine arnica, *Arnica mollis*, brightens the forest with bright yellow blooms throughout the summer. Within a half-hour, complete the gentle descent along rocky outcroppings covered in stonecrop, *Amerosedum lanceolatum*, to reach the tumbling flow of Cataract Creek. Tipperary Lake, 39°48.895' N, 106°19.939' W, is another half-hour along the trail.

From Tipperary Lake, the Gore Range Trail rises within a forty-five minute hike to a junction with the Upper Cataract Trail, where a large cross-cut carved log marks another great spot for a rest and snack. Continue east for a half-hour to Surprise Lake, taking a sharp left turn at the next junction to leave the Gore Range Trail. The final steep descent through lodgepole pines and several meadows to Surprise Trailhead takes a little more than an hour.

A yellow-bellied marmot, *Marmota flaviventris*, prepares her den.

European flax,
Linum usitatissimum.

Northern bedstraw,
Galium septentrionale.

Spotted coralroot,
Corallorhiza maculata.

Yellow stonecrop,
Amerosedum lanceolatum.

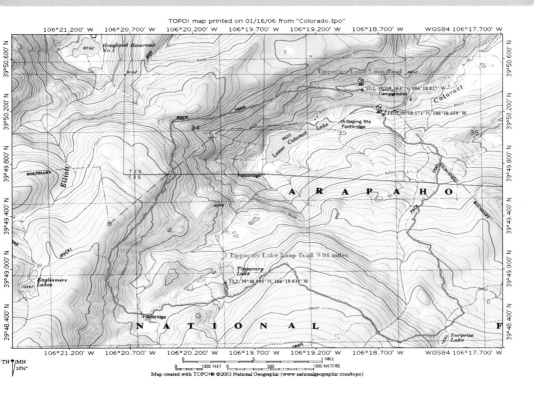

Map created with TOPO! ©2006 National Geographic
http://www.nationalgeographic.com/topo

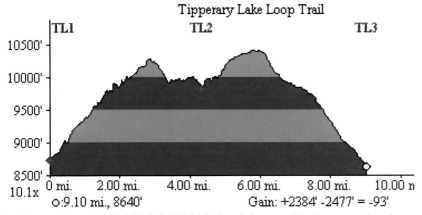

Tipperary Lake Trail begins at an elevation of 8,700 feet and
ascends to 10,250 feet.

Survival Gear

When I meet hikers on wilderness trails in the mountains of central Colo-rado who are wearing shorts, short-sleeved shirts, and running shoes, I am concerned. When they ask me for directions and cannot show me a map, I become worried. When they ask me why I am dressed in ski pants and a fleece on a warm summer day, I laugh.

Anyone who lives in central Colorado knows that a day hike in any season often swings through forty degrees and provides a taste of sunshine, along with a dose of rain, hail, snow, high winds, or any other kind of condition that was not mentioned in the weather forecast. In response to hundreds of miles of hiking through all of the seasons of a day, I have established a fairly constant set of items that fill my day pack in summer and winter.

My list of essentials runs about 25 items, enough survival gear to help me stay alive and probably assist a group of other hikers in the event of a fairly nasty emergency. Since I am almost always alone and hours from rescue, my gear may err on the heavy end. I maintain redundancy in the most im-portant items.

Judging from reported backcountry deaths, I think the most important items are associated with warmth retention and heat generation. I recall the hiker who climbed Longs Peak in shorts and a short-sleeved shirt at the end of August and died of hypothermia. On the other hand, a lone cross-country skier broke a leg near Steamboat Springs and survived more than a week of crawling out by being insulated and, at least for one night, enjoying the heat of a small fire.

Fire is good for heat. Fire may provide some useful work area lighting. Fire may be an emergency signal that can provoke numerous calls to rescue authorities, especially during a dry-season fire ban. A set of three fires is an internationally recognized sign of distress. Fire may also supply water in winter when snow is melted in an empty soup container. However, a hiker who sustains an injury may find it difficult to maintain a fire.

I carry several items associated with heat. I carry a pocket knife in the pocket of my pants to scrape a block of magnesium to ignite tinder. Mag-nesium shavings burn hot and can be lit with sparks from a flint glued to the side of the block. I hang a matchless match, consisting of a magnesium al-loy and a metal striker, and a heavier hunting knife to the outside of my pack with a carabiner for easy access. I carry several cotton balls smeared with petroleum jelly or solid alcohol fuel, such as Sterno®, to generate a flame. Lip balm, comprised primarily of petroleum, may also be used to assist tinder ignition. Matches and fire-starting materials can be stored in waterproof film canisters. The dry understory of a spruce tree often provides the best source for the delicate fibers to initiate a small survival fire.

I carry wooden matches. Wooden matches generate quite a bit of ignition heat and are simple to use. I never carry waterproof matches since I learned several years ago, on a very dark, cloud-covered night, that the wax coating inhibits them from igniting.

GPS fastened to chain link and clasp to ride on top of pack.

Whenever there is snow on trails, I carry several activated charcoal heat packs. Even with insulated boots, layers of socks, and a home-made fleece over-sock, my feet get wet and cold on snowfield ascents. A pair of heat packs under the toes refreshes the blood in the extremities and warms the whole body. Without warm extremities, I can return from a long hike, take a warm shower, and feel a surge of cold, de-oxygenated blood send my body into the severe shakes of mild hypothermia.

For internal heat generation, I carry food to the summits. On sub-zero hikes, I often pack two quarts of hot water in an insulated container and stir packages of hot chocolate into a mug for the high point of a hike. Even on mild winter days, I carry a quart of water for a day hike, fastened by carabiner to the straps on my pack. In summer, I may carry three or four quarts on a hot day. On longer hikes, I will also toss a water filter into the pack, rather than dragging a dehydrated body out of the wilderness at the end of the day.

Layers of fleece are essential for winter adventures. Winter means August on the exposed summits of fourteeners. Cotton shirts soak and chill the body rapidly. Fleece does a fairly good job of wicking perspiration from a climb away from the skin. An outer layer of nylon is essential when the wind blows 70 miles an hour across a mountain ridge a couple thousand feet above the trees.

I spent about $50 on a pair of leather-palm mittens with a breathable nylon upper shell, far better insulation than the rubberized-palm gloves promoted in many outdoor gear shops. When hiking in below-zero conditions, I designed a fleece over-mitt, 18 inches long, to provide protection from powder up to my elbows and an extra layer of insulation. The over-mitt is split in the palm with an escape vent fastened with Velcro to allow finger access. The mittens are not constructed long enough on their own to keep powder out. I dropped the shell down a snow-filled crevice on Fletcher Mountain because I was shaking the snow out. However, they do have a removable fleece glove liner and zipper access along the side of the index finger on the outer shell, which is a handy feature. Aside from my chosen system, the market quickly soars beyond $100 for well-constructed hand protection.

After warmth, I concern myself with the ability to see after dark due to my habit of hiking down trails after sunset. I carry two LED headlamps, one in my pants pocket and the other secured inside my pack on a carabiner. An extra set of lithium batteries, providing approximately 100 hours of extra light, is stashed in a zip-lock plastic bag in one of my pack pockets.

Location is my next priority. I carry a Garmin GPS device loaded with area maps, although the crude 1:100,000 scale often seems inadequate. The GPS goes dead in cold conditions and is not dependable in dense forests. I rigged a chain link to the back panel of the inadequately-engineered back panel, then attached the link to a dog leash clasp on my pack to expose the GPS device to the sky. Reading the GPS display is hopeless after dark, despite the soft glow of an internal display light. For greater breadth and reliability, I carry topographic maps and a compass. In addition, I always pack a few county maps to share with novice visitors.

In the event that I encounter an emergency requiring first aid, I carry a roll of tape and gauze pads. I always pack a scissors to cut clothing away from an injury site or make strips from clothing. Although there is no reception in most areas where I travel, I usually clip my cell phone on the pack to shorten rescue response time if I am able to reach a coverage area. I suggest that you to carry enough survival gear to remain reasonably comfortable through a night that is much colder and darker than the day.

Survival Gear: (Front Row, L to R) 1. lip balm; 2. pocket knife; 3. magnesium fire-starter; 4. matchless match on carabiner; 5. hunting knife; 6. strike matches; 7. scissors; 8. bandages; 9. GPS device with carabiner; 10. topographic map; (Center, R to L) 11. day pack; 12. extra lithium batteries; 13. nylon rope; 14. flagging tape; 15. cell phone with carabiner; 16. compass; 17. LED light with carabiner; 18. backup LED light; 19. heat packs; 20. cotton balls dipped in petroleum jelly; 21. food; 22. water; (Rear, L to R) 23. windbreaker; 24. fleeces; 25. leather palm mitts.

Rock Creek Trail cuts into the heart of the rugged Gore Range.

Rock Creek Trail

Trailhead   39°42.564' N, 106°10.028' W
Destination   39°41.084' N, 106°11.783' W
Hours   2
Miles   4

Locked in the mid-section of the Gore Range is the North Rock Creek watershed, with its pure waters tumbling eastward to meet the Blue River nine miles north of Silverthorne. In summer, the Rock Creek Trailhead provides a popular launching place for adventures into the Eagles Nest Wilderness Area for destinations including Boulder Lake to the north and Willow Lakes to the south. Outdoor enthusiasts including backpackers, hunters, and rock climbers utilize nearly forty dispersed campsites along lower North Rock Creek to prepare for daytime excursions across several dramatically divided alpine watersheds. In winter, Rock Creek Trailhead is sealed a mile below its registry station. Snowshoe and cross country ski tracks are narrow and do not penetrate the depths of the wilderness, allowing absolute solitude to the prepared adventurer.

The junction with Rock Creek Road is at mile-marker 109, along Colorado State Highway 9, north of Silverthorne. On the east side of the highway is Blue River Campground, an outstanding location for summer camping and trout fishing. Turning left, Rock Creek Road ascends for 1.3 miles to a left turn for the winter parking area plowed by Summit County. Past the winter parking area at 9,200 feet in elevation, a narrow and treacherous Forest Service roadway continues for another mile along North Rock Creek to the summer trailhead and parking area, 39°42.564' N, 106°10.028' W. The trek to the trailhead involves an hour on snowshoes or skis.

Continuing west from the trailhead, the entrance to the Eagles Nest Wilderness Area is at an altitude of about 9,500 feet. Within forty-five minutes, the Gore Range Trail crosses the Rock Creek Trail. Proceeding north along the Gore Range Trail for an hour and a half reveals the Boulder Creek watershed and Boulder Lake beyond a ridge at 10,000 feet. Heading south for fifteen minutes from the junction with the Gore Range Trail will allow a view across open willow wetlands at the bridge crossing North Rock Creek. Heading west for about two hours from the intersection with the Gore Range Trail allows access to the site of the abandoned nineteenth century Boss Mine, 39°41.084' N, 106°11.783' W.

The Boss Mine tailings preserve a clearing in the forest that offers views of the abrupt ridgeline rising south of North Rock Creek. One unofficial pathway cuts westward from the Boss Mine along the south face of Keller Mountain for another mile until it vanishes in a young aspen thicket created by recent avalanches. Continuing southwest to a meadow at the upper reaches of North Rock Creek, then scrambling above a small lake at 11,660 feet gives mountain climbers summer access to the summit of Keller Mountain at 13,085 feet. During winter, the ascent to the Boss Mine should be strenuous enough to wear down the energy of most backcountry enthusiasts.

In summer or winter, North Rock Creek offers dramatic scenery.

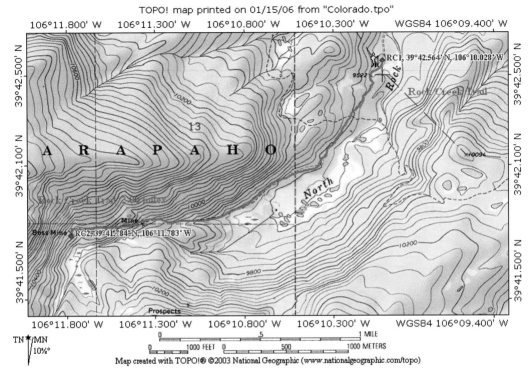

Map created with TOPO! ©2006 National Geographic
http://www.nationalgeographic.com/topo

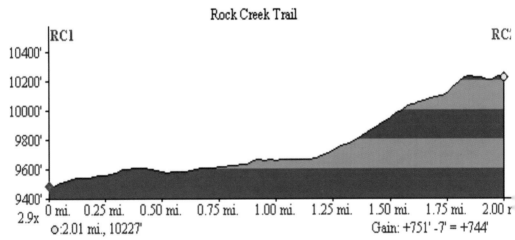

Rock Creek Trail begins at an elevation of 9,500 feet and
ascends to 10,200 feet.

Willow Lakes lie at the base of the jagged spires of Red Peak.

Willow Lakes Trail

Trailhead	39°38.936' N, 106°05.479' W
Destination	39°38.773' N, 106°10.440' W
Hours	5
Miles	6

The Salmon Willow Trail provides moderate hiking access to one of the most dramatic alpine lake areas in the Eagles Nest Wilderness Area of the Gore Range. Willow Lakes are surrounded to the west by a steep, rocky backdrop of peaks rising abruptly nearly two thousand feet above the trail. The hike is a moderately strenuous journey of four hours up to the lakes from the closest access point, with the downhill return taking about two hours. The elevation at Silverthorne is 8,800 feet. Willow Lakes are at 11,400 feet.

From Copper Mountain Village, drive or hop the Summit Stage to the Willowbrook Subdivision in Silverthorne, a left turn about a mile north of the freeway interchange. At the west end of the subdivision, a few hundred vertical feet along Willowbrook Road, 39°38.936' N, 106°05.479' W, find a trail registry at the trailhead parking area developed by Summit County Open Space and Trails.

Enter the trail and proceed north, winding above the housing development for a half hour before turning left at an aspen meadow junction. After turning west, the trail becomes fairly steep with switchbacks rising through lodgepole pine forest to the intersection with the Gore Range Trail in the Eagles Nest Wilderness Area. Note the markings around the intersection, so you come down the southern fork of the trail on the return descent.

Proceed north along the trail. Approximately an hour into the hike, you will come to a junction where the Gore Range Trail crosses North Willow Creek to the left of a large downed spruce that has been cleared from the trail. Do not cross the waterway, but continue northwest beside North Willow Creek.

At two hours into the hike, a wooden trail sign indicates a left turn onto the Salmon Willow Trail for the ascent west, 39°40.056' N, 106°08.883' W. Proceed two hours along the ridge overlooking the watershed of North Willow Creek. Silverthorne, Keystone Resort, and Dillon Reservoir can be viewed in the distance.

If your endurance is wearing thin, take a right turn at a junction a half hour up the trail to the pink rock lining of Salmon Lake. Continue straight ahead, across the boulder field forming the natural dam that holds back the waters of Salmon Lake, and continue ascending to the wetlands of Willow Lakes, 39°38.773' N, 106°10.440' W. Willow Lakes are approximately two miles from the intersection with the Gore Range Trail.

In June, the wetlands are covered in flowers before the drifts of snow dissolve. Wetland crossings are sufficient to keep your feet dry in most seasons. However, snow cover may obscure the trail in spots from December through the end of June. North Willow Creek cascades through several steep cataracts from Willow Lakes down to the ravine where it meets water draining from Salmon Lake. To the south, the ragged sky-piercing chutes of Red Peak arise, shutting winter sunlight from Willow Lakes.

North Willow Creek is lined with marsh marigolds, *Psychrophila leptosepala*.

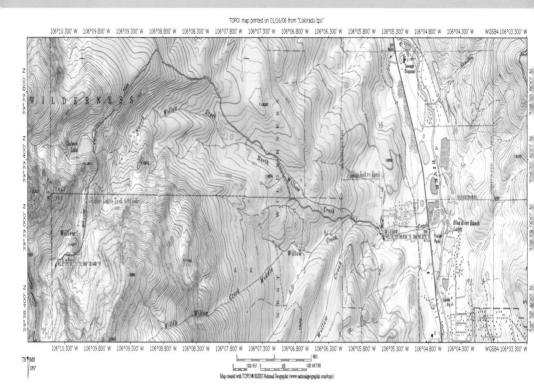

Map created with TOPO! ©2006 National Geographic
http://www.nationalgeographic.com/topo

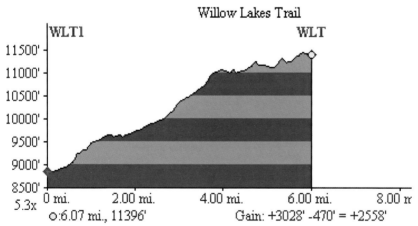

Willow Lakes Trail begins at an elevation of 8,800 feet and
ascends to 11,400 feet.

The Gore Range Trail passes Buffalo Mountain to reach South Willow Falls.

South Willow Creek Trail

Trailhead	39°37.074' N, 106°06.666' W
Destination	39°37.769' N, 106°08.220' W
Hours	3
Miles	6

The Eagles Nest Wilderness Area is comprised of 134,000 acres of upland lodgepole pine, spruce, fir, and aspen forest in northern Summit and Eagle counties, with tundra above the tree-line at approximately 11,500 feet. The eastern slope of the Gore Range, the mountains protected within the boundaries of the Eagles Nest Wilderness Area, extend from Silverthorne north to Heeney within Summit County. Summit County provides a dozen major trailhead access points for hiking and horseback riding along more than forty miles of the Gore Range Trail.

The Summit Stage provides a free bus ride to some of the best hiking trailheads in the county for those without access to a vehicle. The Summit Stage leaves Frisco for Silverthorne every half hour. After the ten-minute ride to Silverthorne, the Wildernest Route of the Summit Stage leaves for Wildernest.

For those who want spectacular scenery without the price of substantial climbing, try starting at Buffalo Mountain Trailhead in Wildernest. Silverthorne is at about 8,800 feet, but Buffalo Mountain Trailhead is starts at around 9,800 feet. Within five hours of hiking, you can make an arc around Buffalo Mountain, climb to South Willow Falls at the base of Red Mountain, and drop down to the Willowbrook Trailhead.

After registering at Buffalo Mountain Trailhead, 39°37.074' N, 106°06.666' W, hike north through the lodgepole forest for about forty-five minutes to a junction. Going straight will take you to South Willow Creek.

Within an hour, you will follow a drainage ditch to a large clearing and cross a rock field. After two hours of hiking north, you will drop into a couple hundred feet of muddy wetland. Beyond the wetland, there are four log bridges across South Willow Creek before the junction with the Gore Range Trail.

At the junction, turn left to climb about a half-hour to South Willow Falls, 39°37.769' N, 106°08.220' W. Tumbling cataracts provide a great backdrop for lunch. Descend east along the Gore Range Trail to the junction with the Mesa Cortina trail. Along the way, you will pass open wetlands along South Willow Creek, with views of Buffalo Mountain and Red Peak.

Take a right turn, back across South Willow Creek. Proceed a few hundred feet, looking for a trail descending to the left. Follow that trail into the ravine along the south side of South Willow Creek until you find a log bridge to cross over to a Summit County Open Space and Trails sign on the north side of the stream. The Summit County trail will take you north across Middle Willow Creek and North Willow Creek to the Willowbrook Trailhead. Once there, descend along the subdivision road for twenty minutes to catch the next Summit Stage.

Rock break fern, *Pteris vittata.*   Brittle fern, *Cystopteris protrusa.*

Clustered lady's slipper,
Cypripedium fasciculatum.

Golden aster,
Chrysopsis villosa.

Mountain goldenrod,
*Solidago multiradiata
scopulorum.*

Pontilla shrub,
Pontilla fulgens.

Parry lousewort,
Pedicularis parryi.

Spotted coralroot,
Corallorhiza maculata.

Meadow rue,
Thalictrum polygamum.

Twisted stalk,
Streptopus lanceolatus.

Sweet cicely,
Myrrhis odorata.

Death camas,
Anticlea elegans.

White bog orchid,
Limnorchis dilitata albiflora.

Daisy,
Erigeron elatiar.

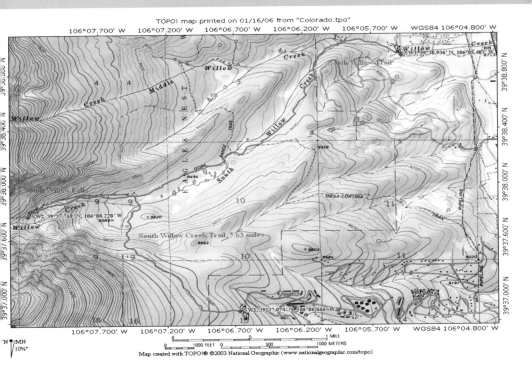

Map created with TOPO! ©2006 National Geographic
http://www.nationalgeographic.com/topo

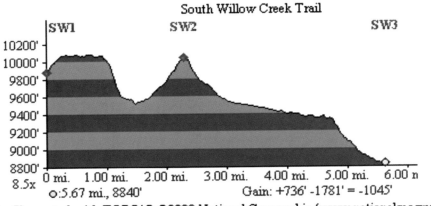

South Willow Creek Trail begins at an elevation of 9,800 feet and
ascends to 10,100 feet.

The Buffalo Mountain Trail follows the eastern ridge of Buffalo Mountain.

Buffalo Mountain Trail

Trailhead	39°37.218' N, 106°06.598' W
Destination	39°36.951' N, 106°08.569' W
Hours	4
Miles	6

Buffalo Mountain is one of the most visible promontories of Summit County, being situated immediately north of Frisco at the gap that marks the southern end of the Gore Range. Looking like a fattened herbivore curled on its side beneath a covering of winter snows, Buffalo overlooks Silverthorne, Dillon, Keystone, and Frisco. From its summit, Buffalo allows a great perspective on the Ten Mile Range to the south, twin fourteeners Grays and Torreys to the southeast, and the Ptarmigan Wilderness Area beyond the Blue River along the corridor running north.

The Buffalo Mountain Trail rises from the ruins of a mining era cabin on the east face of Buffalo Mountain, north of Salt Lick Gulch. In order to reach the Buffalo Mountain Trail, drive up Ryan Gulch Road through Wildernest, west of Silverthorne. At about 9,800 feet, a trailhead registration display marks the Buffalo Cabin Trailhead beside the Ryan Gulch wetland area.

Within twenty minutes of hiking, the boundary marker of the Eagles Nest Wilderness Area should be visible along this well-traveled and nearly-level trail. After thirty minutes, take a left turn at the junction with the trail that continues north to South Willow Creek. After a dozen minutes, an opening with a large snowdrift marks the site of the ruins of a mining cabin.

The trail begins a rapid climb from around 10,200 feet, freeing itself from the tracks of casual cross-country skiers. Snowshoes are useful along this stretch of trail through the woods, preventing post-holing to the hip where the tender snow pack may crumble away. Tremendous views of Dillon Reservoir and Tenderfoot Mountain, with Grays and Torreys rising beyond, are possible from several vantage points among the trees.

At two hours out, the tree-line should quite suddenly open at about 11,000 feet to a forty-five degree slope of snow dotted with a few rock cairns that mark the summer trail switchbacks. After enjoying the view over a cup of hot chocolate, cast aside the snowshoes and start digging toeholds into the hard pack for a steep vertical ascent, up and west at about sixty degrees. The false summit at about 12,000 feet gives a more gradual ridgeline climb for the half-mile hike southwest to the true summit at 12,777 feet.

The sunset views from above tree-line are a spectacular reward for a strenuous day of struggling up snow-covered slopes. In the northwest, Red Peak raises its ragged head. Northeast, the Williams Fork Mountains provide a broad display of equal heights. The slide down the snowfields at dusk is notably more pleasant than the ascent.

For More Information:

Virtual Dillon Ranger District, Buffalo Mountain trail and map description, http://dillonrangerdistrict.com/summer/bufcab_hkgtpo.htm.

Hawkweed,   Rosy pussytoes,
Hieracium albiflorum.   *Antennaria microphylla.*

TOPO! map printed on 01/16/06 from "Buffalo[1].tpo"

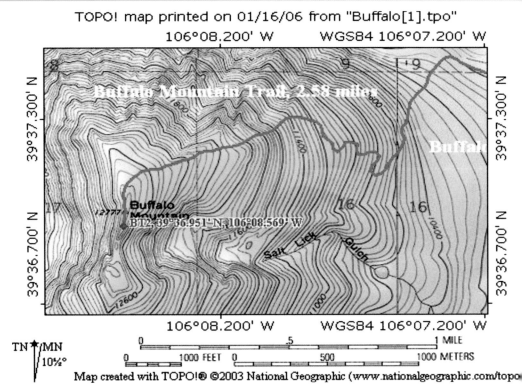

Map created with TOPO! ©2006 National Geographic
http://www.nationalgeographic.com/topo

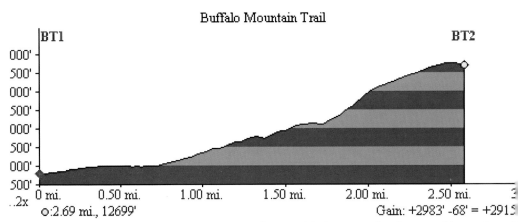

South Willow Creek Trail begins at an elevation of 9,800 feet and
ascends to 12,777 feet.

Lily Pad Lake rests north of Frisco and the Tenmile Range.

Lily Pad Lake Trail

Trailhead	39°37.140' N, 106°06.630' W
Destination	39°36.030' N, 106°06.962' W
Hours	1
Miles	2

Nestled among a dense lodgepole pine forest at the southeast edge of the Eagles Nest Wilderness Area, the Lily Pad Lake Trail offers easy access to great views of the Blue River Valley surrounding Dillon Reservoir. With an elevation gain of only 200 feet and length of 2 miles, Lily Pad Lake Trail is a welcome path for a family trek in hiking boots, snowshoes, or cross-country skis. No mountain biking is permitted and pets should be leashed beyond the wilderness boundary.

The trailhead begins on the eastern face of Buffalo Mountain in the Wildernest development, a few miles above Silverthorne. In order to reach the trailhead area by public transit, hop on a Wildernest Summit Stage from the bus transfer station near the Silverthorne Post Office, west of Highway 9 north at Third Street.

By personal vehicle, take the Silverthorne exit from I-70 and turn left at the first intersection on Highway 9 north of the freeway. Begin traveling west along Wildernest Road, the frontage access wrapped around the base of Buffalo Mountain. Follow the switchbacks by turning right onto Ryan Gulch Road. Proceed through the Wildernest condominium for 3.6 miles to the shared parking pad for the Buffalo Mountain Trail and Lily Pad Lake Trail.

The lower trailhead is the entry to the Buffalo Mountain Trail that climbs 3,000 feet to the northwest to reach the summit of Buffalo Mountain. Up the road a hundred steps, beyond the Summit Stage bus stop, is the gated Forest Service Road that serves as the trailhead for the Lily Pad Lake Trail.

The Lily Pad Lake Trail, 39°37.140' N, 106°06.630' W, at 9,830 feet, follows the topography to the south. About forty minutes, the Lily Pad Lake Trail meets the Salt Lick Trail, 39°36.327' N, 106°06.815' W, at 10,010 feet, where the trail turns to the right and follows a water diversion ditch. The trail continues through a wetland area where moose are frequently sighted. In a bit over an hour, the trail reaches fraternal twin ponds, Upper Lily Pad Lake and Lower Lily Pad Lake, before descending to the Meadow Creek Trailhead near Frisco.

Upper Lily Pad Lake is a shallow pond covered in yellow water lilies, *Nuphar lutea sub. polysepala,* in summer and frequented by ducks. Across a small earthen berm, Lower Lily Pad Lake, 39°36.030' N, 106°06.962' W, provides a view of the north end of the Tenmile Range above the lodgepole forest. To the north, the summit of Buffalo Mountain rises above the shoreline.

Beyond the beaver dam that helps close the outlet to the lake, the trail drops through open meadows and aspen glens filled with wildflowers in summer. After a snack near the lakes, the trek back along the same trail returns to the parking area. An alternative adventure continues south to the junction with the Meadow Creek Trail and descends into Frisco. A short walk along a gravel frontage road leads across the freeway overpass to the Summit Stage transfer center in Frisco, where a free bus to Silverthorne can be found.

For More Information:

Virtual Dillon Ranger District, Lily Pad Trail map and description, http://dillonrangerdistrict.com/summer/lilpad_hkg.htm.

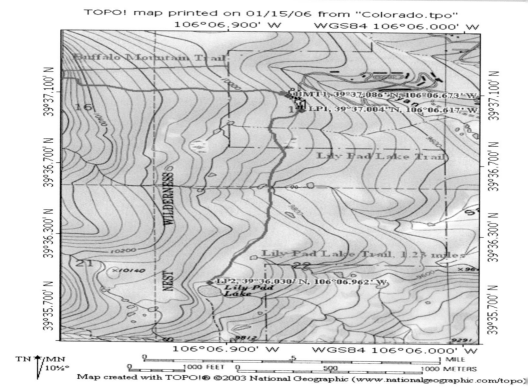

Map created with TOPO! ©2006 National Geographic
http://www.nationalgeographic.com/topo

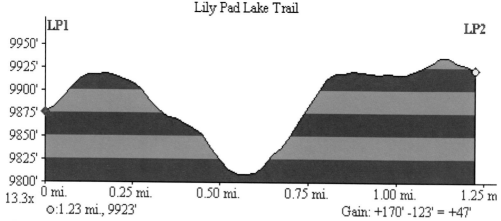

Lily Pad Lake Trail begins at an elevation of 9,830 feet and
ascends to 10,101 feet.

The Meadow Creek Trail overlooks Dillon Reservoir below Lily Pad Lake.

Meadow Creek Trail

Trailhead   39°35.338' N, 106°06.359' W
Destination   39°36.490' N, 106°10.313' W
Hours   6
Miles   10

Few locations in Summit County provide more beautiful overlooks of Dillon Reservoir and the surrounding mountains than Meadow Creek Trail north of Frisco. Across open aspen meadows, the lower switchbacks of Meadow Creek Trail allow views of Mount Royal and Ophir to the South and, beyond the frozen water of Dillon Reservoir, Swan, Tenderfoot, Grays, and Torreys in the East.

In order to begin exploring the Meadow Creek Trail, head north from Frisco along Summit Boulevard, cross the freeway beyond the transit center and shopping mall, take the frontage road leading west from the roundabout where the bronze elk stands. At the end of the frontage road lies the Meadow Creek Trailhead, 39°35.338' N, 106°06.359' W. After registering at the Forest Service display, climb along the southern bank of Meadow Creek and pass the ruins of a long-abandoned cabin.

Within a half-hour of beginning the ascent, the trail opens onto clearings that provide excellent views of the surrounding area. A few feet beyond the aspen meadows, the trail is swallowed by dense lodge pole pine forest. At the first junction, proceed straight ahead to follow the ravine west into the wilderness along Meadow Creek.

One hour into the climb, cross Meadow Creek and proceed through the lodge pole on the north side of the stream at an elevation of about 10,000 feet. Another hour into the hike, the forest opens, revealing Buffalo Mountain to the north and Chief Mountain to the south. The trail crosses Meadow Creek again at 11,000 feet.

Continuing its westward gain, the trail crosses Meadow Creek a third time at 11,200 feet before beginning a steep ascent to merge with the Gore Range Trail at Eccles Pass, 39°36.490' N, 106°10.313' W, altitude 11,900 feet. With breaks for refueling, assuming snow conditions do not create an impasse, plan five hours to complete the task and four hours to return to the trailhead. From Eccles Pass, look north to Red Peak with a summit of 13,189 feet and steep chutes that block the winter sun from reaching Willow Lakes immediately beyond. In the valley before Red Peak lies the South Willow Creek watershed. The Gore Range Trail heads north through Eccles Pass and drops eastward along South Willow Creek, past South Willow Falls, on the north side of Buffalo Mountain with its summit at 12,777 feet.

For More Information:

Virtual Dillon Ranger District, Meadow Creek Trail map and description, http://dillonrangerdistrict.com/summer/meacre_hkg.htm.

Pinedrops,
Pterospora andromedea.

Watsons penstemon,
Penstemon watsonii.

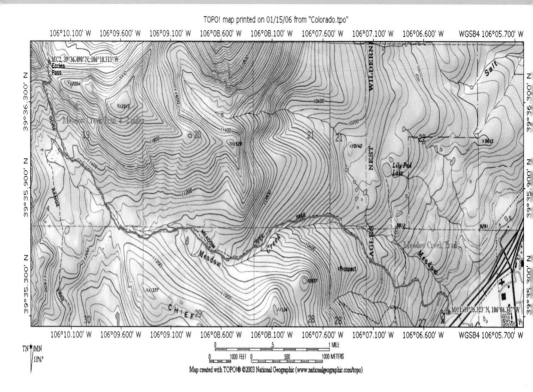

TOPO! map printed on 01/15/06 from "Colorado.tpo"

Map created with TOPO! ©2006 National Geographic
http://www.nationalgeographic.com/topo

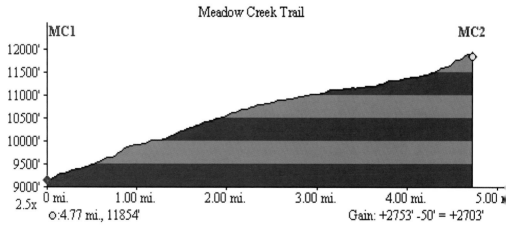

Profile created with TOPO!® ©2003 National Geographic (www.nationalgeographic.com/topo)

Meadow Creek Trail begins at an elevation of 9,100 feet and ascends to 11,900 feet.

Red Buffalo Pass blends the dappled colors of snow, meadow, and pines.

North Tenmile Creek Trail

Trailhead	39°34.561'N, 106°06.821' W
Destination	39°36.490 N, 106°10.313 W
Hours	7
Miles	12

When seeking high places with great overlooks in Summit County, few paths can match the beauty and diversity of North Tenmile Creek Trail and its merger with the Gore Range Trail. The North Tenmile Creek Trail rises west from a parking pad at the junction of Interstate 70 and Main Street at the outskirts of Frisco, 39°34.561'N, 106°06.821' W, at an altitude of 9,160 feet, heading upstream to meet the Gore Range Trail for a steep ascent north past Chief Mountain to Eccles Pass. A loop back along the Meadow Creek Trail to the north will provide ten hours of hiking pleasure to fill an entire day.

The North Tenmile Trail gradually rises west for the first hour to a sign marking the boundary of the Eagles Nest Wilderness Area. Along the way, hikers pass meadows dappled in spruce and filled with peavine, asters, and mouse ear. After entering the wilderness, the trail narrows and continues rising gently for the next mile to the junction with the Gore Range Trail.

Turning north, the Gore Range Trail rises steeply along several switchbacks from 10,000 feet in the ravine to an 11,000 foot plateau of lodgepole pines west of Chief Mountain. Along the trail, visitors may find white and red paintbrush, along with bunches of Parry clover, *Trifolium parryi*. At four hours into the hike, the trail passes along the peaceful shoreline of a highland brook and spring-fed bog, excellent settings for a rest.

Within another half-hour, the lodgepole forest opens to the large open bowl of the Meadow Creek watershed. After crossing Meadow Creek at 11,400 feet, 7 miles from the North Tenmile Creek Trailhead, the Gore Range Trail meets the Meadow Creek Trail. The Gore Range Trail proceeds north past a small cluster of avalanche lily, *Erythronium grandiflorum*, glowing yellow petals marking the pathway north to Eccles Pass.

The final ascent to Eccles Pass follows switchbacks, arriving at ridge elevation of 11,900 feet, 39°36.490 N, 106°10.313 W. Looking north from Eccles Pass, Red Buffalo Pass slices the sky to the left to separate South Willow Creek from the Gore Creek watershed. Across the gap, Red Peak, 13,189 feet, provides a steep and jagged wall sheltering the Willow Lakes lying to its north. The Gore Range Trail continues east to South Willow Falls.

Buffalo Mountain rises in the east at 12,777 feet along the ridge from Eccles Pass. Among the craggy cliffs of Eccles Pass, alpine wildflowers cover the rock ledges. Enjoy the carpet of blooms including sky pilot, *Polemonium viscosum*; Parry lousewort, *Pedicularis parryi*; alpine Smelowskia, *Smelowskia calycina*; spotted saxifrage, *Saxifraga bronchialis*; moss campion, *Silene acaulis subacaulenscens*; and alpine forget-me-not *Eritrichum aretioides*. After exploring Eccles Pass, return to Frisco along Meadow Creek or North Tenmile Creek, an easy descent of about three hours.

Parry clover,
Trifolium parryi.

Avalanche lily,
Erythronium grandiflorum.

Parry lousewort,
Pedicularis parryi.

Alpine smelowskia,
Smelowskia calycina.

Spotted saxifrage,
Saxifraga bronchialis.

Moss campion,
Silene acaulis subacaulescens.

Alpine forget-me-not,
Eritrichum aretioides.

Sky pilot,
Polemonium viscosum.

Goldeneye,
Heliomeris multiflora.

Subalpine buckwheat,
Eriogonum subalpinum.

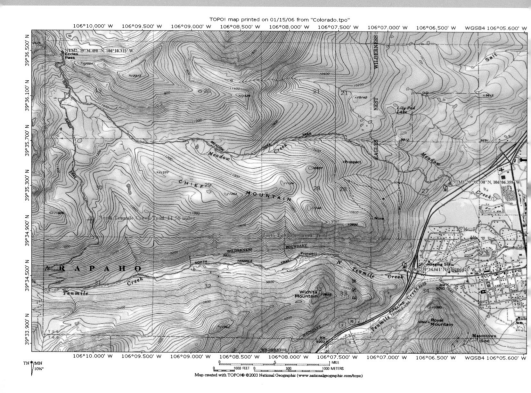

Map created with TOPO! ©2006 National Geographic
http://www.nationalgeographic.com/topo

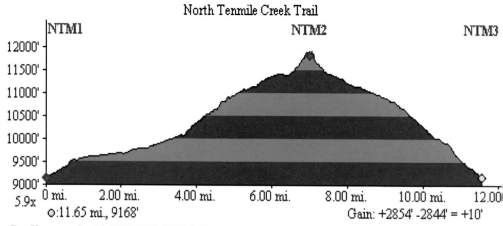

Profile created with TOPO!® ©2003 National Geographic (www.nationalgeographic.com/topo)

North Tenmile Creek Trail begins at an elevation of 9,160 feet
and ascends to 11,900 feet.

Wheeler Lakes lie calmly beneath a brooding autumn storm.

Wheeler Lakes Trail

Trailhead	39°31.039' N, 106°08.808' W
Destination	39°31.209' N, 106°10.089' W
Hours	3
Miles	6

Copper Mountain is fortunate to be located immediately south of the Eagles Nest Wilderness Area. Many miles of remote snowshoe and cross-country ski experience is accessible along the Gore Range Trail, with the trail to Wheeler Lakes beginning across the freeway from Copper Mountain Village. The official entry registration site is along the wetlands located a half-mile east of Copper Mountain at the scenic area turn-out, 39°31.039' N, 106°08.808' W. However, visitors to Copper Mountain can walk across the freeway overpass and begin ascending west through the snowdrifts at the interchange ramp, 39°30.570' N, 106°08.524' W.

During the winter months, the journey to Wheeler Lakes may be characterized as strenuous. If descending the groomed slopes at Copper Mountain is losing its challenge, try a day of ascending from 9,600 feet to 11,800 feet at Uneva Pass, three miles to the north, through knee-deep powder.

From the overpass, follow the freeway west for a quarter-mile, along a nearly level trail across the freeway from East Village. Then, proceed across a meadow where the signs of foraging elk should be visible. The trail turns up a steep ravine, with a break in the spruce trees allowing views of Center Village and the slopes at Copper Mountain. An hour above the freeway, the trail crosses a stream at the boundary of the Eagles Nest Wilderness Area. A downed log at the wilderness boundary, elevation around 10,200 feet, provides a good resting area to down a pint of water and a high-energy snack to fuel the next segment of the trek.

Continuing north for another hour should reveal an open wetland covered in willows at a junction in the trail. The trail to the north proceeds to Wheeler Lakes within a half-hour, rising to a ridgeline at 11,200 feet that provides a view northeast over Officers Gulch to Dillon Reservoir in the distance.

The trail to the west is the Gore Range Trail that levels off and continues north for more than forty miles to Grand County. An hour farther along the Gore Range Trail, a two-hour descent may be made along the north side of the main stream channel to reach Officers Gulch Pond at the freeway interchange two miles north of Copper Mountain. Two hours north of Wheeler Lakes, Uneva Pass provides views overlooking North Tenmile Creek. For a full-day adventure, a five-hour descent from Uneva Pass into the North Tenmile watershed provides an exit to Main Street in Frisco, with Summit Stage bus service back to Copper Mountain.

For More Information:

Virtual Dillon Ranger District, Wheeler Lakes Trail map and description, http://www.dillonrangerdistrict.com/summer/whefla_hkg.htm.

In winter, Wheeler Lakes rest under a blanket of snow above Officers Gulch.

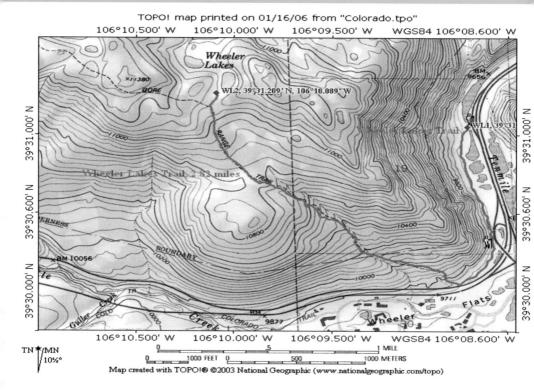

Map created with TOPO! ©2006 National Geographic
http://www.nationalgeographic.com/topo

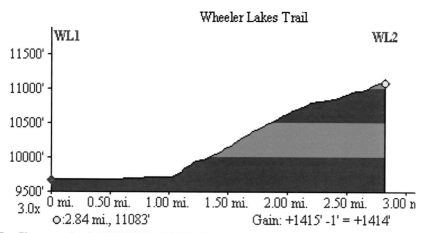

Wheeler Lakes Trail begins at an elevation of 9,700 feet and
ascends to 11,200 feet.

Alpine ponds above Officers Gulch overlook Tenmile Canyon to the south.

South Gore Range Trail

Trailhead	39°30.417' N, 106°08.689' W
Destination	39°34.524' N, 106°06.837' W
Hours	7
Miles	14

The Gore Range Trail extends 45 miles from Grand County to Copper Mountain. It coincides with the trail up to Wheeler Lakes west of the exit ramp from I-70 for Copper Mountain Village. Parking is available at the rest area a half-mile before the exit ramp or at the Wheeler Trail parking area at the end of the eastbound frontage road across Highway 91 from Copper Mountain Village. The Summit Stage drops passengers at the entrance to Copper Mountain Village, allowing a short walk north across the freeway overpass to the Gore Range Trail.

The Gore Range Trail, beginning at an elevation of 9,720 feet, 39°30.417 N, 106°08.689' W, follows the freeway west for a half-mile. In summer, blooming sagebrush, cinquefoil, and pussytoes line the trail. The trail turns north, rising through a ravine filled with aspen, lodgepole pine, blue spruce, and fields filled with lupine.

The entry to the Eagles Nest Wilderness Area is about a mile up the trail, 39°30.379' N, 106°09.324' W, at 10,150 feet. After a stream crossing, the trail continues north past a wilderness entrance sign. The trail winds farther uphill into a large willow meadow. The Wheeler Lakes Trail branches off to the right 2.6 miles from the trailhead, 39°31.110' N, 106°10.150' W, at 11,040 feet. The Gore Range Trail continues northwest along a ridge, passing large blue spruce trees before opening onto a meadow with views west to Wilder Gulch. The slopes of Copper Mountain, 12,441 feet, Union Mountain, 12,313 feet, and Jacque Peak, 13,205 feet, can be seen through the trees to the south.

Two ponds are nested above Officers Gulch, a mile past the junction with the Wheeler Lakes Trail, 39°31.393' N, 106°11.012' W, at 11,365 feet. The ponds are about two hours from the beginning of the trail. Another hour of hiking reveals Lost Lake near Uneva Pass, 5.2 miles into the hike, 39°32.179' N, 106°11.017' W, at 11,620 feet. The lake rests near tree line, at the base of a colorful red mound south of Uneva Peak, 12,522 feet.

Continue north and steeply up the slope past Lost Lake to reach Uneva Pass.
After four hours of hiking, climb to the highest point at Uneva Pass, 39°32.745' N, 106°11.033' W, at 11,970 feet, about 6.8 miles into the hike. To the northeast is Wichita Mountain, 10,855, south of the point where North Tenmile Creek pours into the Town of Frisco. A few minutes later, pass to the right of a small pond and descend into the forest. After many descending switchbacks, the trail crosses North Tenmile Creek and meets the North Tenmile Trail to Frisco, 10.2 miles into the hike.

Begin the final 4 miles of the hike by turning right and following the North Tenmile Trail east, descending to the trailhead at 9,413 feet. The entire 16 mile hike can be completed in 6.5 hours. The Summit Stage stops at the Frisco Town Hall for the return trip to Copper Mountain Village.

Lost Lake south of Uneva Pass overlooks Jacque Peak.

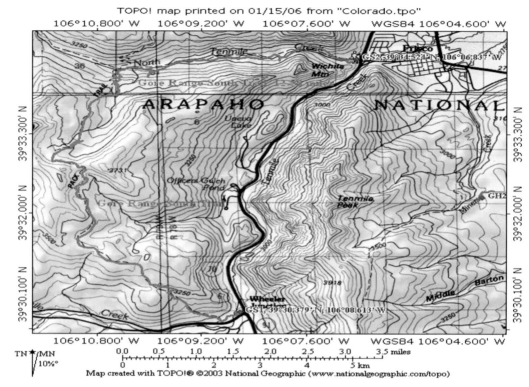

Map created with TOPO! ©2006 National Geographic
http://www.nationalgeographic.com/topo

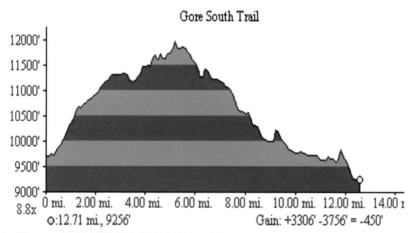

Gore Range Trail South begins at an elevation of 9,700 feet and
ascends to 11,620 feet.

Leave No Trace

In 1965, hikers and backpackers in the United States totaled an estimated 10 million. By 1999, the number of hikers and backpackers grew to nearly 98 million, with an estimated 26 million campers at dispersed campsites. With this growth in visitors to public lands, the damage to natural resources is becoming more noticeable. Compacted, barren soils in primitive campsites, deeply eroded hiking trails, scattered trash, fire rings filled with broken glass, motorized vehicle damage, and unburied human waste are a few of the problems observed by visitors to public lands.

Responding to the increased impact of visitors on natural resources, land managers identified a set of principles that reduce the detrimental effects of increases in outdoor recreation. Applying good judgment with concern and respect for natural resources is the goal of these Leave No Trace ideas. The seven principles of Leave No Trace that guide outdoor recreation are: Plan Ahead; Travel and Camp on Durable Surfaces; Dispose of Waste Properly; Leave What You Find; Minimize Campfire Impacts; Respect Wildlife; and Be Considerate of Other Visitors.

Planning ahead means packing food in containers appropriate for the quantities necessary for the proposed trip and utilizing reusable containers that are packed out from remote areas. Minimizing the weight of packaging and reducing the quantity of products carried into campsites or developed campgrounds reduces trash disposal requirements. Know the regulations concerning the use of fires, establishing campsites away from water sources and trails, and occupation by vehicles, pets, or livestock in the specific areas visited.

Broken glass, crushed cans, molten plastic, and other trash accumulate inside unsightly rock rings constructed by abusive campers. Rock rings damage natural resources and form hazards to public safety.

Limiting campsites and travel to durable surfaces is not always possible. However, every traveler can avoid trampling sensitive wetland areas. Try to not widen hiking trails by walking single-file and staying in the center of trails. Climb up and over logs that block trails rather than trampling detour paths around obstacles. When establishing a campsite, either camp on soils already compacted or camp far from existing impact areas, away from lakes, streams, and trails, without digging or cutting green vegetation.

Waste disposal starts with waste reduction. Those who drag a case of beer bottles into a wilderness campsite, then toss empty bottles into a bon-fire all night long are not practicing a Leave No Trace ethic. Carry an extra trash bag along when hiking to pack out your own waste as well as that generated by those lacking awareness.

Bury human waste under a few inches of soil or beneath dead and down tree falls. Count at least fifty steps from trails and waterways before creating a campsite. Carry wash water far from streams and lakes.

Leave what you find, except for damage by others. Do not pick an armful of blue columbine blossoms while wandering through aspen meadows. Do not construct furniture or a rock fire ring at your primitive campsite. Do not break all of the branches from the conifers or sagebrush within sight of your campsite.

Minimize the use of fires. Build no more of a fire than you can burn to coals within a half hour. Use sticks that you can break by hand, not larger diameter wood that will not be consumed to ashes. Watch your campfire until you extinguish any remaining coals, detour any behavior that requires containing the flames with rocks. Build a mound or container fire and avoid sterilizing the soil beneath your fire. Turn under or disperse ashes. Pack an isopropyl alcohol burner, about the size of a coffee cup, or multi-fuel backpacking stove to eliminate the need for a cooking fire.

Respect wildlife by not occupying riparian corridors, essential access routes for nearly every creature in the forest. Keep dogs on leash to prevent the harassment of wildlife and other visitors. Do not encourage wildlife dependency on visitor food waste. Out of respect for others, do not bring radios, fireworks, and other noise makers into developed campgrounds or more primitive areas. In every aspect of conduct, try to remain invisible to others. Minimize both your visual and audible footprint.

While these brief tips for Leave No Trace recreation are not comprehensive, applying the basic principles to guide all of your behaviors while enjoying the outdoors will minimize your impact on the natural resources that are shared by a growing number of visitors to our public lands each year. By minimizing damage to our natural resources and avoiding conflicts with other users, you ensure the enjoyment of wild areas for future generations and reduce the need for area closures or other restrictions on the freedom to fully enjoy the natural resources that all of us share as stewards.

For More Information:

Leave No Trace principles,
http://www.lnt.org/programs/lnt7/

The trail from Deluge Creek east to Buffalo Pass is a great mid-summer destination.

Gore Creek Trail

Trailhead	39°37.637' N, 106°16.484' W
Destination	39°37.350' N, 106°10.612' W
Hours	8
Miles	14

Gore Creek drops out of the Eagles Nest Wilderness Area from a watershed extending north to Willow Peak, at 13, 357 feet, and east to Red Buffalo Pass. Gore Creek Trail provides access to a diverse span of wetland areas along approximately six miles of pathway that begins at Gore Creek Campground at East Vail. The trail is moderately difficult with an elevation gain from 8,680 feet to 11,400 feet at Gore Lake.

In order to find the entry point to the Gore Creek Trail, travel west from Summit County to Exit 180 at East Vail. Proceed under the interstate and turn left, heading southeast along Bighorn Road for a little over two miles. The trailhead parking area is to the left of Gore Creek, before the entrance to Gore Creek Campground. Ascend from the registration site and bear right along the trail at the junction with the Deluge Lake Trail.

Hollygrape, *Mahonia repens.*

Subalpine larkspur, *Delphinium barbeyi.*

Snowball saxifrage, *Saxifraga rhomboidea.*

Dainty subalpine blooms thrive in the spray of Deluge Creek.

The first mile of trail is often busy with locals walking dogs. Dogs should be leashed within the wilderness area. Since the Eagles Nest Wilderness Area is a primitive preserve, no bicycles are permitted on the trail. Solitude soon captures the trail above the first few aspen meadows. Along the way, hikers can enjoy looking down into a gorge of turbulent water.

About two miles along the trail, Deluge Creek drops down from the north to join Gore Creek. An unofficial trail ascends abruptly to the left, creating a scramble up Deluge Creek. Do not be deceived by this crumbly, precipitous tread, unless looking for a scenic overlook to Red Buffalo Pass. Snowball Saxifrage, Micranthes rhomboidea, blooms in a moist bed along Deluge Creek, along with other tiny subalpine flowers.

The Gore Creek trail turns right and crosses Deluge Creek a few feet down elevation across a rough-hewn log, then continues east along Gore Creek. Above Deluge Creek, the trail becomes a stream in the early season or during a storm. Beaver ponds line the trail and provide some relief to the flooding. Among the beaver ponds and wet meadows, Cornhusk Lily, *Veratrum tenuipetalum*, arises with its large poisonous leaves.
Water diversion bars are needed along the steep ascent to assist the trail in shedding its rivulets tumbling over gravel trail beds to Gore Creek.

White Globeflower, *Trollius albiflorus*, is a white buttercup that enjoys wetland areas along Gore Creek. The yellow flowers of Hollygrape, *Mahonia repens*, are very common in the drier Montane areas among the lodgepole pines overlooking Gore Creek.

After five miles of climbing, the Gore Creek Trail offers a choice of steep climbs up to Gore Lake, to the north, or to the winding switchbacks of Red Buffalo Pass, to the east, where it joins more than forty miles of the Gore Range Trail.

White globeflower, *Trollius albiflorus*, is a member of the buttercup family that enjoys wetland areas along Gore Creek.

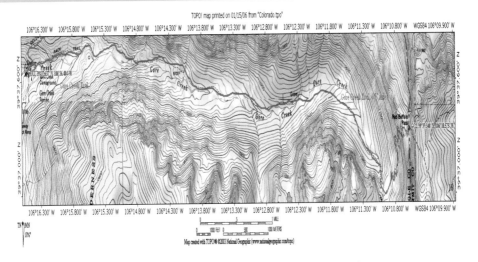

Map created with TOPO! ©2006 National Geographic
http://www.nationalgeographic.com/topo

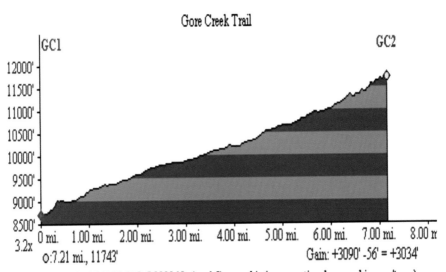

Profile created with TOPO!® ©2003 National Geographic (www.nationalgeographic.com/topo)

Gore Creek Trail begins at an elevation of 8,680 feet and rises to
11,400 feet at Gore Lake.

Looking east from the Deluge Lake Trail, the rugged Gore Range cuts the sky in a sunset alpenglow.

Deluge Lake Trail

Trailhead	39°17.637' N, 106°16.484' W
Destination	39°39.354' N, 106°13.679' W
Hours	6
Miles	12

As autumn daylight becomes ever more stunted, the blooms of summer fade in the high country. Shrubs along mountain trails struggle to bear the weight of darkening berries. Bears feast on the bounty in preparation for the long winter fast. Pika and other burrowing animals trim the rock garden flora to add extra lining to their nests as evening temperatures drop toward freezing and clouds darken the sky with threats of the first snowfall. Mosquitoes and biting flies retreat, allowing muffled footfalls to supplant the whining as the only sounds along deep wilderness trails.

Now is the ideal time to climb above the aspen and fir to wish the mountains a peaceful rest through the winter months when the depths of the wilderness become impenetrable. Among the high destinations, the Deluge Lake Trail provides an opportunity to pass by meadows filled with berries and rise to view the last blooms of the season framing the high country streams. From the trailhead, Deluge Lake is a rigorous climb of 5.68 miles into the Gore Range.

Serviceberry,
Amelanchier arborea.

Mountain gooseberry,
Ribes inerme.

Hollygrape,
Mahonia repens.

Subalpine daisy,
Erigeron peregrinus.

The Deluge Lake Trail rises out of East Vail. Driving west from Summit County, take the East Vail turn-off, Exit 180, turning left under the freeway. Proceed east 2.5 miles along Bighorn Road to the trailhead parking area along the west side of Gore Creek. The Deluge Lake Trail breaks away to the left from the Gore Creek Trail at a junction 0.2 miles above the trail register.

Beyond the entrance to the Eagles Nest Wilderness Area, subalpine daisies, *Erigeron peregrinus*, cover the slopes among the aspen groves with lavender blossoms and dust gentle bumblebees with pollen. False forget-me-nots, mint, mountain chimes, cinquefoil, fireweed, and goldenrod complete the orchestra of flowers fading to seed. Rock outcrops along the steep switchbacks of the trail provide views of Vail to the south across the valley.

The Deluge Lake Trail rises quickly from 8,600 feet at the trailhead to 9,210 feet within the first hour. Through dense stands of berries among the aspen, the trail ascends over Gore Creek. Here, serviceberry bushes, *Amelanchier arborea*, provide a bountiful food supply for bears attempting to gain weight before the onset of winter. Mountain gooseberry, *Ribes inerme*, also lines the trail as it winds among the aspen and ancient spruce. Higher, among the dense lodge pole pines, hollygrape, *Mahonia repens*, provides a ground cover of darkening fruits.

Harebell,
Campanula rotundifolia.

Pearly everlasting,
Anaphalis margaritacea.

Two hours along the trail, at 10,480 feet, wetlands in the dense forest shield yellow arnicas and the pastel blooms of wild geraniums. The trail breaks briefly into open rock sprays, with dramatic drops to the rushing Gore Creek a thousand feet below. Then, the ascent becomes more gradual. After three hours of hiking, 4.5 miles into the hike, the trail gently levels off and follows Deluge Creek up the gulch to the northeast at about 10,800 feet.

The pale royalty of the harebell, *Campanula rotundifolia*, hang like guardians to the trail. Tiny white clusters of the pearly everlasting, *Anaphalis margaritacea*, also brighten the fields along the way. In the wetlands, the dark blue blooms of the star-shaped larkspur, *Delphinium nelsonii*, a member of the Buttercup Family, grow as tall as 6 feet. Nearby, the tusks of the little red elephant, *Pedicularis groenlandica*, of the Figwort Family, grow stunted along the brooks.

The Deluge Lake Trail crosses Deluge Creek and continues to rise in elevation to the tree line. As the spruce trees diminish in size among the meadows, large patches of rosy paintbrush, *Castilleja rhexifolia*, mark the path. Views of the rocky amphitheater surrounding Deluge Creek are unimpeded by forest at this high altitude and the mule deer are forced to buck hundreds of feet across the fields to seek cover.

After four hours of climbing, the trail reaches a crest 3,172 feet above the trailhead and drops to the lakeshore at 11,690 feet. Drifts of snow on the steep rocky slopes continue to melt into Deluge Lake throughout the summer season. Beside the icy water of the lake, the porcelain blooms of alpine primrose, *Primula parryi*, and stiff red-topped stems of rose crown, *Clementsia rhodantha*, brighten the shore. Peering southwest from the outlet of Deluge Lake, the summit of Red Benchmark, at 11,816 feet, is visible beyond thick bundles of the deathwatch blooms of summer.

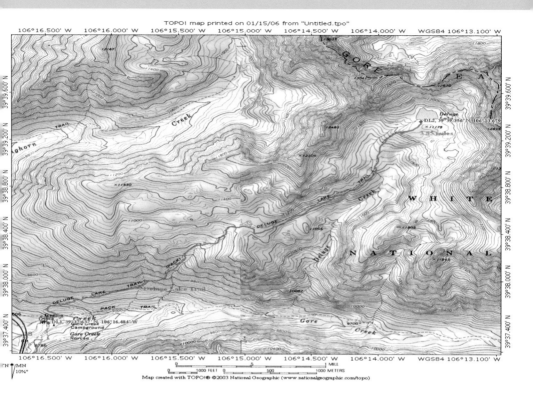

Map created with TOPO! ©2006 National Geographic
http://www.nationalgeographic.com/topo

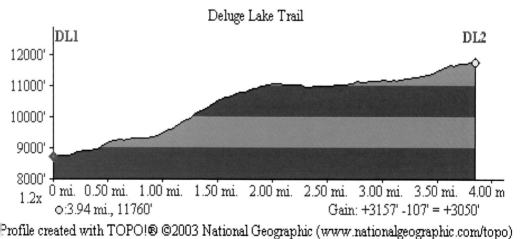

Deluge Lake Trail begins at an elevation of 8,600 feet and
ascends to 11,690 feet.

Sunset generates a bronze glow on the avalanche chutes near Pitkin Falls.

Pitkin Lake Trail

Trailhead   39°38.628' N, 106°18.175' W
Destination   39°41.590' N, 106°17.303' W
Hours   6
Miles   10

The Gore Range oddly received its name from a hunting expedition led by Jim Bridger, 1804-1881, early trapper and explorer of the Rocky Mountains. Bridger documented the Great Salt Lake in 1824 and guided westward settlers through Bridger Pass in 1850, shortening the Oregon Trail by 61 miles. During the mid-nineteenth century, the flow of settlers divided and diminished the great herds of American buffalo and caused starvation among the native tribes occupying the Great Plains.

In 1854, Sir George Gore hired Bridger as a hunting guide out of Fort Leavenworth, Kansas. The Gore expedition traveled through the central Colorado mountain range before heading north into the Yellowstone area. Gore practiced a policy of heavy treading on the land, hauling 30 wagons and more than 50 servants on his expedition of 6,000 miles. Gore shot thousands of large game animals during his guided tour of the mountains that extended into 1855. Later, in 1859, Bridger led a surveying group through the Yellowstone area.

The Gore Range extends from Grand County in the north to Copper Mountain in the south, with many watersheds divided by steep and rugged mountain ridges. Near the middle of the western slope of the Gore Range is the Pitkin Creek valley.

The Pitkin Creek Trail is found 17 miles west of Copper Mountain on I-70. At East Vail, Exit 180, take a right turn on the north frontage road to the trailhead parking pad, 39°38.578' N, 106°18.186' W. Pitkin Creek Trail crosses Pitkin Creek and ascends rapidly during a 3 hour hike from 8,400 feet to Pitkin Lake, 39°41.590' N, 106°17.303' W, at 11,390 feet, deep in the Eagles Nest Wilderness Area.

In winter, a blanket of silence surrounds the trail within an hour of the trailhead, with nothing marking the trail except the tracks of an elk that wandered along the banks of Pitkin Creek. With knee-deep powder covering the trail, expect a pace of 1 mile an hour.

The avalanche chutes along the eastern ridge drop from the boundary between Eagle and Summit counties and form the frozen flow of Pitkin Falls about 3 miles from the trailhead. Pitkin Lake is 5 miles up the ravine at the base of the main summit of Eyrie Horn, 13,041 feet. Beyond the ridge east of Pitkin Lake, 5 miles up the ravine, are South Slate Creek and Boulder Creek watersheds in Summit County.

The hike is a rigorous round trip of 10 miles to Pitkin Lake and back to the trailhead. The tread is firm on the 3,000 foot descent, with great views of Vail Resort at Red Benchmark, 11, 816 feet, and the Holy Cross Wilderness Area beyond.

Elk trails criss-cross the snow covered willows along Pitkin Creek.

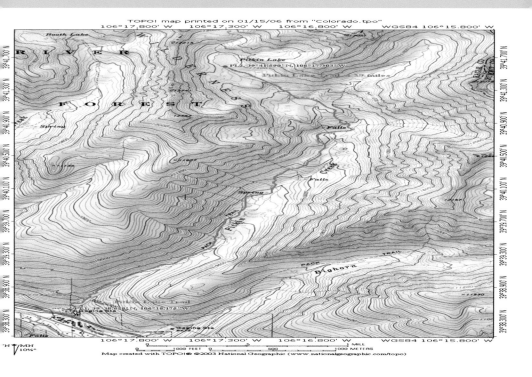

Map created with TOPO! ©2006 National Geographic
http://www.nationalgeographic.com/topo

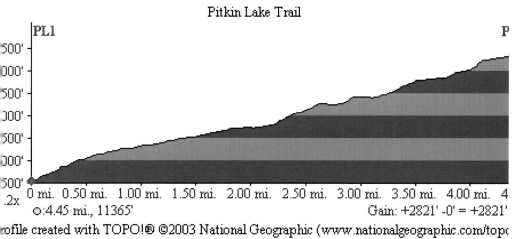

Pitkin Lake Trail begins at an elevation of 8,4000 feet and
ascends to 11,400 feet at Pitkin Lake.

A limestone escarpment dominates the view east of Booth Creek.

Booth Creek Trail

Trailhead   39°38.983' N, 106°19.191' W
Destination   39°41.924'N, 106°18.254' W
Hours   6
Miles   12

Whether you are up for a cold-water kayaking experience this spring or a wildflower hunting expedition this summer, Booth Creek Trail may satisfy your desires. Located on the meeting of the granite structure of the Gore Range and the limestone escarpment of the Vail Valley, the Booth Creek Trail offers dramatic rock outcroppings, waterfalls, and an alpine lake along its six-mile length.

Booth Creek Trail ascends six miles and 3,000 feet from East Vail, at 8,400 feet, to Booth Lake, elevation 11,480 feet. Although the trail is arduous at times, the rewards are diverse. Access the trailhead from Summit County by taking the East Vail exit from Interstate 70. Travel west along the north frontage road for about a mile, watching for the Booth Falls Trailhead about two-tenths of a mile north of the freeway.

During the early spring, Booth Creek Trail snow cover is only packed down for the first two hours of climbing to an altitude of approximately 9,500 feet. After the spring thaw, a kayak, wetsuit, helmet, technical climbing equipment, and courage precipitate offer a chance for a challenging paddle at 10,000 feet, through the upper rapids, Booth Falls, and beyond. The upper gorge, above Booth Falls, provides several small drops to challenge those who are not daring enough to plunge more than sixty feet over the falls.

For those with a longer life expectancy, Booth Creek Trail offers a great opportunity in the calmer quest for summer wildflowers. The trail climbs among aspen meadows filled with wildflowers along the first mile. Keep a watchful in the dry meadows for the scarlet trumpet, *Gilia aggregata*. This distinctive foot-high stem holds brilliant red, five-point trumpets favored by hummingbirds along its stem.

In these grassy meadows, also look for scarlet paintbrush, *Castilleja miniata*, meaning colored red. The sturdy spikes hold bracts of double-lobed flowers ranging in color from purple to sunset pink. Paintbrush is hemiparasitic, drawing nutrients from the roots of adjacent plants.

In the darker conifer forest above Booth Falls, look in more shaded areas of fertile soil along the stream banks for dark purple lobes of monkshood. A poisonous plant, Monkshood sap was used by early hunters to poison arrowheads. *Aconitum dephinifolium*, also known as wolfbane, is a member of the buttercup family.

Among the cool, sheltered rock formations along Booth Creek search for the blooms of Columbine. The Blue columbine, *Aquilegia caerulea*, is the state flower of Colorado. Columbine is named after the Latin for dove, *columba*, for its delicate winged petals that often hover over pools of water. Native Americans utilized the ground seeds of the Columbine as an aphrodisiac to charm women. If the Monkshood does not kill you and the Columbine fails to mesmerize you, complete the hike along the shores of Booth Lake, at 11,476 feet, nestled among the steep rocky slopes of Twin Towers and Eyrie Horn in the Gore Range.

Colorado columbine,
Aquilegia coerulea.

Rosy paintbrush,
Castilleja rhexifolia.

Monkshood,
Aconitum columbianum.

Fairy trumpet, *Gilia aggregata.*

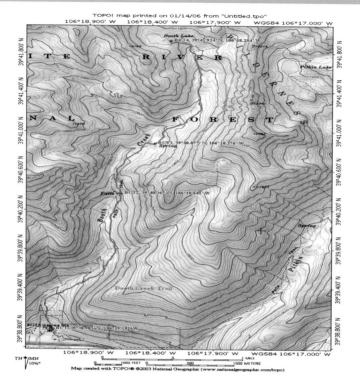

Map created with TOPO! ©2006 National Geographic
http://www.nationalgeographic.com/topo

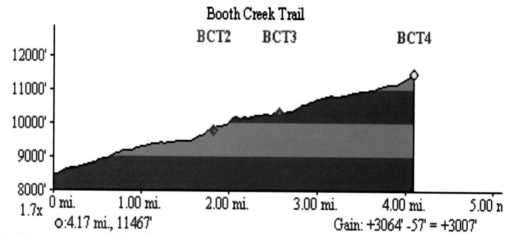

Booth Creek Trail begins at an elevation of 8,400 feet and
ascends to 11,480 feet at Booth Lake.

At the entrance to Eagles Nest Wilderness Area, Piney Lake provides a restful shoreline beneath the rugged peaks of the northern Gore Range.

Upper Piney Trail

Trailhead   39°43.210' N, 106°24.306' W
Destination   39°44.154' N, 106°21.700' W
Hours   4
Miles   7

The features of a great casual hike in the Eagles Nest Wilderness Area may include an alpine lake, frothy waterfalls, wildflowers in season, and a rugged backdrop of mountain peaks. The Upper Piney Trail provides easy access to all of these on a round-trip hike of about eight hours.

From Copper Mountain, the Upper Piney Trailhead is a drive of 33 miles. The drive takes a little more than an hour. The first half of the trip is on the I-70 west to Vail Exit 176, west along the frontage road for a mile, then north along Red Sandstone Road for another mile. On the second leg of the journey, take Forest Service Road 700, a gravel road, north for ten miles to the Piney Crossing Trailhead parking area, 39°43.210' N, 106°24.306' W.

Hike east to the Upper Piney Lake Trail junction along the north side of Piney Lake, elevation about 9,342 feet. Roaming upstream five miles, Upper Piney Trail gains about 1,000 feet in elevation, making this a fairly easy trek for the Gore Range.

In summer, the aspen meadows along Piney River are filled with the blooms of red columbine, *Aquilegia elegantula*; lambstongue groundsel, *Senecio integerrimus*; lovage, *Ligusticum porteri*; common harebell, *Campanula rotundifolia*; and wild rose, *Rosa woodsi*. Foaming waterfalls are a little less than three miles upstream at an elevation increase of only 430 feet, 39°44.154' N, 106°21.700' W. The hike to the waterfall is a casual walk for hikers of almost any age and ability.

Looming eastward above the cataracts are Meridian Peak, Mount Powell, and the Lions Throne. As the trail rises to the south toward Upper Piney Lake, the Kehlstein, 12,005 feet; Twin Towers, 12,692 feet; and Eyrie Horn, 13,041 feet, reveal themselves above the stream.

Adventurous explorers may follow the social trails that lead east and scale the summit of Mount Powell. Continue south along the main trail to Upper Piney Lake, a hike of seven miles, 2,000 feet above the trailhead. Regardless of the final destination of this hike, be sure to pack out trash and leave no more impact than essential to enjoy the heights of this wandering path in the wilderness.

The Twin Towers, summit elevation of 12,692 feet, provide a beautiful backdrop to the winding course of Upper Piney River.

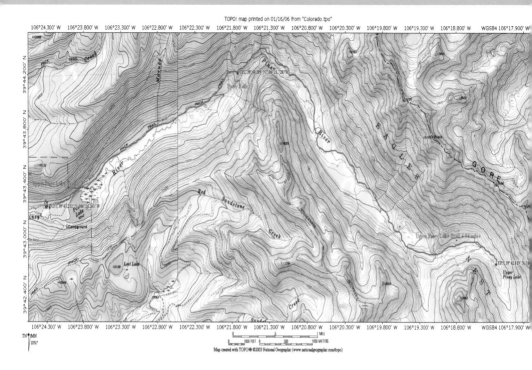

Map created with TOPO! ©2006 National Geographic
http://www.nationalgeographic.com/topo

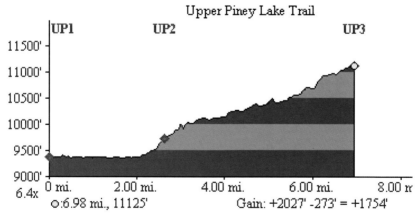

Profile created with TOPO!® ©2003 National Geographic (www.nationalgeographic.com/topo

Upper Piney Trail begins at an elevation of 9,340 feet and
ascends to 11,370 feet at Upper Piney Lake.

Mountain goats graze on the south slopes of the Continental Divide.

Deer Creek Trail

Trailhead	39°34.256' N, 105°51.616' W
Destination	39°31.681' N, 105°51.741' W
Hours	5
Miles	8

The Continental Divide separates the North American continent into two great watersheds, flowing to the east or west from the tundra-covered mountain tops of eastern Summit County. For a taste of the Continental Divide at the southeastern edge of Summit County, explore the historic mining area surrounding Deer Creek.

Follow the Snake River upstream along Highway 6 to Keystone, then turn south on Montezuma Road, Summit County Road 5, and ascend 7 miles to the village of Montezuma. Montezuma is a mining town that was settled around 1863 during a major silver boom. Remnants of mining operations from more than a century ago dot the mountain slopes surrounding the community. Beyond the little village are deteriorating roads slicing the sides of the valleys to provide access to the Upper Snake River and the Deer Creek watershed, tributary to the westward flowing Snake River. Heading south of Montezuma, Webster Pass Road forks to the east or left, while Deer Creek Road climbs straight south.

Deer Creek is a multi-use area where cross-country skiers, all-terrain vehicle operators, mountain bikers, and hikers can begin a trek in any season from parking pads near Montezuma and continue south up a gradually ascending high-clearance rocky road following the banks of Deer Creek. Mileage is meaningless in this area where top speeds with an all-wheel drive vehicle are measured in low first gear revolutions of the wheels during the dry weeks of summer. However, marking the climb at 3 miles is a reasonable estimate, giving an hour for each mile of touring by any means of transportation. An adventure up to the Continental Divide should be an average outdoor experience for Summit County, about three hours up and two hours down.

The Deer Creek valley is an open willow-filled meadow surrounded by lodge pole pines and the barren rock face of Glacier Mountain along the western slope. From the base at 10,500 feet, the trail rises to about 12,200 feet at the junction with the Radical Hill Jeep Trail to the east and the Middle Fork Road to the Swan River heading west. Saints John Road crosses Glacier Mountain to the northwest, with the Gore Range forming the distant horizon.

Climbing east to the spine of Teller Mountain at 12,615 feet, along the Continental Divide, Park County lies to the south along the North Fork of the South Platte River. Red Cone, 12,801 feet, stands brightly lit to the east. Webster Pass Road descends from 12,100 feet into Handcart Gulch, immediately west of Red Cone. The twin peaks of Grays and Torreys form the northern line of the Continental Divide at the edge of Clear Creek County.

Rare tundra floral species, such as sea pink, *Armeria maritima sub. sibirica*, occupy the fragile scree fields along the Continental Divide near Hoosier Pass. Therefore, tread lightly along existing paths and roadways. In the quietude of these high places, scan the sun dappled southern slopes for mountain goats foraging among tufts of grasses.

> Webster Pass Road descends along the base of Red Cone into Handcart Gulch in Park County.

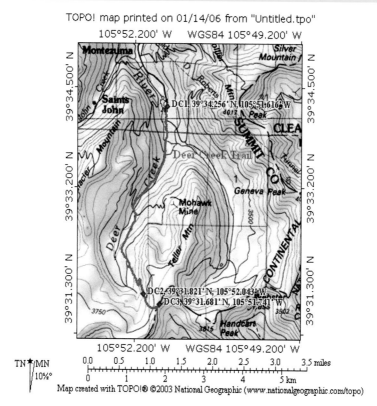

TOPO! map printed on 01/14/06 from "Untitled.tpo"

Map created with TOPO! ©2006 National Geographic
http://www.nationalgeographic.com/topo

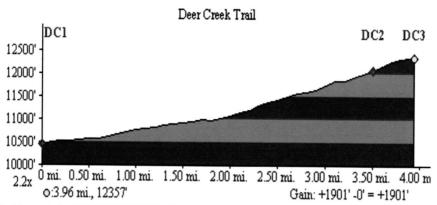

Deer Creek Trail

Deer Creek Trail begins at an elevation of 10,500 feet and
ascends to the Continental Divide at 12,200 feet.

Grays Peak, 14,270 feet, and Mount Edwards, 13,850 feet, form the Continental Divide east of Torreys Peak.

Grays Peak Trail to Torreys Summit

Trailhead	39°39.661' N, 105°47.065' W
Destination	39°38.566' N, 105°49.274' W
Hours	6
Miles	8

Grays and Torreys Peaks are distinctive and spectacular for being part of the great wall of North America, the Continental Divide, dividing the land into eastern and western watersheds. Water falling on the north-facing slopes of Grays and Torreys Peaks flows north into Quale Creek, then blends with Clear Creek and descends eastward to the Front Range. Chihuahua Gulch gathers water from the south side of Torreys Peak and Peru Creek takes water from the southeast slopes of Grays and the west side of Argentine Peak, delivering the precious lode to the westward-flowing Snake River.

The Grays Peak Trail provides an easy approach to the twin Fourteeners marking the eastern edge of Summit County. Plan to spend 7 hours on the trail to reach the summit, enjoy the views, and complete the descent to the parking area. The trailhead is 16 miles east of Silverthorne, south of the Bakersville interchange on I-70. Forest Service Road 189 provides fairly smooth access to the trailhead for vehicles that clear a few water diversions and rocks along the way.

The Grays Peak Trail begins 3 miles above the freeway, 39°39.661'N, 105°47.065' W, at 11,200 feet. The summit of Torreys Peak is 4.15 miles from the trailhead, 39°38.566' N, 105°49.274' W. During the first hour of the hike, the trail ascends south through the wetland willows of Stevens Gulch. The trail passes between Stevens Mine on a lower slope of McClellan Mountain, 13,587 feet, forming the eastern wall of the valley, and Sterling Silver Group Mine beside the trail to the right on Kelso Mountain, 13,164 feet. The trail climbs 900 feet during the first 1.7 miles to a reassuring National Recreation Trail sign asserting that the summit of Grays Peak is only 2 miles farther.

The trail divides after 2.5 hours and 3 miles of climbing among the tumble of rocks on the north slope of Grays Peak. Along the way, anticipate the possibility of encountering a pika or mountain goat on the trail. The junction, 39°38.271' N, 105°48.794', separates the eastern approach to the summit of Grays Peak from a lateral trail across several avalanche chutes to the saddle at the base of Torreys Peak. At 13,330 feet, the lateral trail provides a more gradual ascent of 570 feet to the saddle. Be prepared for high winds and cold conditions on the northern slope of the mountain.

From the saddle between Grays and Torreys, the views are spectacular. Stevens Gulch is spread below to the northeast. The slopes of Keystone Mountain, 11,641 feet, North Peak, 11,661, and South Peak, 11,982, seem to be a short hike to the west, with Dillon Reservoir sparkling in the distance beyond. Grays Peak, 14,270 feet, and Mount Edwards, 13,850 feet, form the ridge that is the Continental Divide east of Torreys Peak.

The final ascent to the summit of Torreys Peak, at 14,267 feet, is steep and reduces the hiking pace to half-steps. The summit of Torreys Peak is approximately 4 hours from the trailhead, while the descent requires only 2.5 hours. If time remains in the day, cross the saddle and climb to the top of Grays Peak before taking the winding trail back into Stevens Gulch.

The slopes of Keystone Mountain, 11,641 feet, North Peak, 11,661, and South Peak, 11,982, from the summit of Torreys Peak.

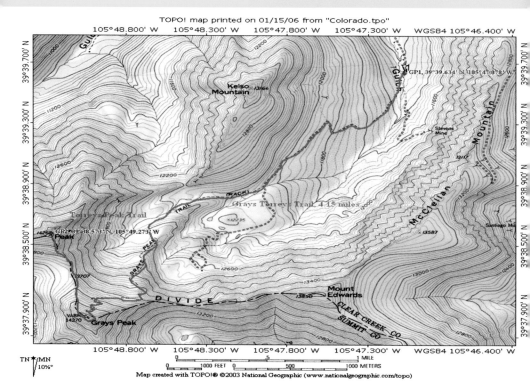

Map created with TOPO! ©2006 National Geographic
http://www.nationalgeographic.com/topo

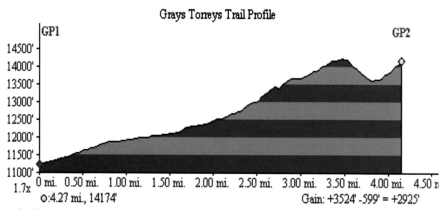

Grays Peak Trail begins at an elevation of 11,200 feet and
ascends to Grays Peak, 14,270 feet and Torreys Peak, 14,267 feet.

Hypothermia

Hypothermia is the potentially life-threatening condition where the body loses core temperature, impairing the processing of chemicals and diminishing both muscular and mental functions. Outdoor enthusiasts in an alpine environment need to protect against this condition and be especially aware of the signs of hypothermia onset.

The human body is designed to process chemical reactions at 98.6 degrees. When any part of the body drops below that temperature, cells are unable to eliminate lactic acid and perform other essential metabolic functions. The central nervous system can restrict blood flow to the extremities of the body by a magnitude of 100 times when the external environment threatens the core temperature.

Every year, backcountry recreation kills several people in Colorado. The common causes of these tragedies are dramatic temperature fluctuations, insufficient layers of clothing, fatigue, dehydration, insufficient food intake, lack of heat sources, and dampness.

The symptoms of the onset of hypothermia include shivering, loss of coordination, and restriction of blood flow to the extremities leading to cold hands and feet. Five degrees of loss in core body temperature, considered moderate hypothermia, leads to violent shivering, slurred speech, and diminished judgment. Severe hypothermia, the loss of ten degrees of core temperature, causes periodic shutdown of shivering, stiff muscles due to the accumulation of lactic acid, dilation of the pupils, and dangerous restriction of breathing and heart rate.

Prevention and treatment of hypothermia includes reduction of heat loss by carrying sufficient layers of clothing such as insulated pants, water-wicking fleece, an extra pair of dry socks and gloves, and a windbreaker. Periodic supplementation of calories, taking breaks every hour to drink hot chocolate or cider, eat sweet snacks, and consume protein for the long-haul, restores energy needed to heat the body and water to assist metabolic processes. After the onset of hypothermia, the addition of heat by fire or other sources should focus on the body core to prevent surges of cold, de-oxygenated blood from the extremities to overwhelm the body before normal metabolism is restored.

Masontown mining ruins remain at the base of Mount Royal.

Mount Royal Trail

Trailhead	39°34.488' N, 106°06.653' W
Destination	39°33.957' N, 106°06.721' W
Hours	3
Miles	4

Winter blesses the high country with generous drifts of snow. Snow makes mountain trails challenging, but not entirely impassible. Focusing on lower-altitude pathways allows good conditioning and scenic adventures even during the depths of the winter season.

One such hike that can be an easy round-trip of three miles to the ruins of a mining settlement is the Mount Royal Trail at the southern edge of Frisco. If trail conditions permit, the Mount Royal Trail continues for another mile to a summit overlook with views east of Dillon Reservoir and north through the lower Blue River Valley. The hike to the summit generally takes an hour-and-a-half, with another hour for the descent.

From the I-70 westbound from the Eisenhower Tunnel, take the second exit for Frisco, Exit 201, and drive under the interstate onto Main Street. Before reaching the shops of Main Street, take a right turn into the parking area beside the interchange. A sign board, grill, and picnic table greet visitors along the shore of North Tenmile Creek, 39°34.488' N, 106°06.653' W, at an elevation of 9,145 feet.

Cross North Tenmile Creek and follow the paved recreation path east to skirt the cliffs of Mount Royal. An interpretive display describes the settlement of Masontown and marks the footpath that ascends the mountain. Turn right, heading south, just short of a half-mile from the parking area. The cabin and factory ruins are one mile upslope, 39°33.958' N, 106°06.147' W, at an elevation of 9,495 feet, and can be reached at a brisk walking pace.

In 1872, the Masontown Mining and Milling Company built a cyanide-leach process extraction operation for silver and gold on the side of Mount Royal. A small settlement of cabins surrounded the factory with peak employment exceeding one hundred working five primary tunnels. However, the mining venture went bust by the turn of the century. In 1912, the abandoned reduction mill was destroyed by an avalanche. Similarly, the remaining cabins along the sides of the gulch were swept away by avalanche slides in 1926.

Beyond the lower mining ruins, the Mount Royal Trail continues west on a steeper incline for another mile to the summit. At 10,230 feet, the trail splits. Climbing straight ahead eventually leads to the summit of Peak 1, 12,805 feet, and Tenmile Peak, 12,933 feet. The trail to the right ascends north to the summit of Mount Royal, 10,502 feet, 39°33.957' N, 106°06.721' W.

From the summit, a cliff faces the Gore Range in the Eagles Nest Wilderness Area. Ptarmigan Peak Wilderness Area in the Williams Fork Range rises beyond Buffalo Mountain in the northeast. The North Tenmile watershed winds through the valley in the west. Looking east, the twin fourteeners, Grays and Torreys, point skyward beyond the Dillon Reservoir and Keystone Ski Resort.

The summits of Grays and Torreys can be seen east of Mount Royal.

TOPO! map printed on 01/15/06 from "Colorado.tpo"

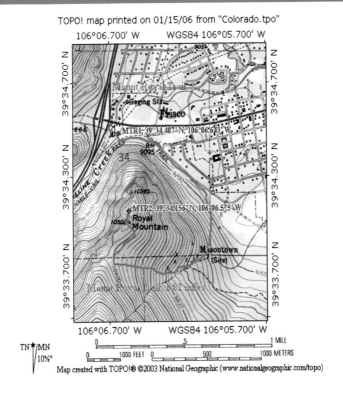

Map created with TOPO! ©2006 National Geographic
http://www.nationalgeographic.com/topo

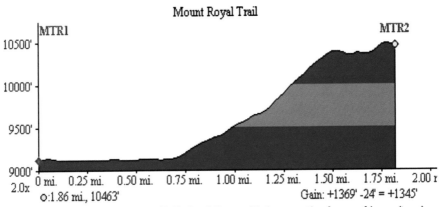

Mount Royal Trail begins at an elevation of 9,145 feet and
ascends to the summit at 10,502 feet.

Bistort, *Bistorta bistortoides.*

Golden banner, *Thermopsis divaricarpa.*

Gold Hill Trail

Trailhead	39°32.443' N, 106°02.560' W
Destination	39°32.256' N, 106°04.922' W
Hours	3
Miles	6

The hot days of summer may inspire the search for easy hikes of short duration. Convenient to Breckenridge and Frisco, the Gold Hill Trail may be the perfect fit for an afternoon climb in the pursuit of wildflowers. With more reserve energy, Gold Hill Trail provides access to a section of the Colorado Trail that can take you all the way to Copper Mountain and destinations farther west over the Tenmile Range.

The Gold Hill Trail is located south of Frisco, only a mile past the intersection of Highway 9 and Swan Mountain Road. The trailhead parking is a right turn from the north, about a half mile before the intersection with Tiger Road. Gold Hill Trail ascends west from 9,216 feet, crosses a ridge one mile south of Ophir Mountain, reaching a maximum elevation of around 10,230 feet before dropping down to Miners Creek. The distance round trip is 6.25 miles, which can be covered in three hours.

Gold Hill Trail provides a few overlooks through clearings in lodgepole forest to view the tips of North and South Peak at Keystone to the east as well as Swan Mountain and glimpses of Dillon Reservoir to the north. The trail is lined with beds of wild strawberries and violets. The white cylinders of bistort, *Bistorta bistortoides,* and blossoms of golden banner, *Thermopsis divaricarpa,* fill open meadows recovering from timber harvests made in 1988, demonstrating the diversity of growth that is possible when homogeneous lodgepole stands are broken. Within the damp ravine within the lodgepole, white flowers of mouse ear, *Cerastium beeringianum earlei*, can be seen among tall stands of cornhusk lily, *Veratrum tenuipetalum.*

At the terminus of the short hike, the rewards include views of Tenmile Peak, Peaks 3 through 5, across a beaver pond at the junction joining the Peaks Trail. A large patch of mountain bluebells, *Mertensia ciliata,* blanket the banks of Miners Creek with a profuse display of drooping blue blossoms.

For more extensive adventures, several alternative routes exist beyond the Gold Hill trail. Continuing south on the Peaks Trail provides a pathway to Cucumber Gulch in Breckenridge, several miles south of Gold Hill. A few minutes of hiking downhill from the trailhead offers the Peak 8 Base with a Town of Breckenridge bus stop for service to the downtown or a Summit Stage ride north to Tiger Road. Turning west on the Miners Creek Trail allows a crossing of the Tenmile Range between Peak 5 and 6 to merge in a steep descent along the Wheeler Trail to Copper Mountain with Summit Stage service back to Frisco.

A wildland fire burned a small area of lodgepole pine trees and high desert sage meadow south of Ophir Mountain in September, 2005. The fire was suppressed by local structural firefighters and Forest Service personnel.

Alpine mouse ear, *Cerastium beeringianum earlei.*

Mountain bluebell, *Mertensia ciliata.*

TOPO! map printed on 01/15/06 from "Colorado.tpo"

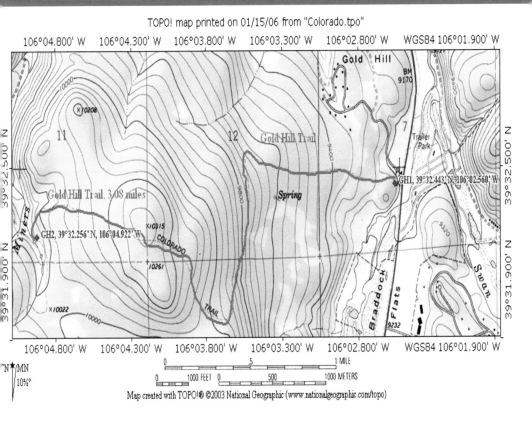

Map created with TOPO! ©2006 National Geographic
http://www.nationalgeographic.com/topo

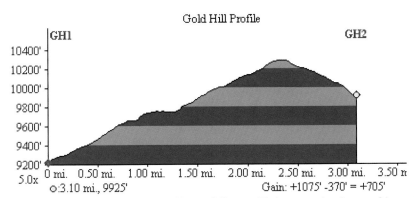

Gold Hill Trail begins at an elevation of 9,216 feet and
ascends to the summit at 10,230 feet.

The Wheeler Trail overlooks Officers Gulch in Eagles Nest Wilderness Area.

Wheeler Trail

Trailhead	39°30.552' N, 106°08.536' W
Destination	39°34.322' N, 106°05.111' W
Hours	8
Miles	14

When he grazed cattle at the base of Copper Mountain around 1880, Judge John S. Wheeler used a trail on the side of the Tenmile Range to get his stock over the mountains before snowfall. Today, that route extends about 14 miles from Copper Mountain to the south end of Summit County at Hoosier Pass. A junction with the Miners Creek Trail on the west face of the Tenmile Range allows passage south, forming a 14.4 mile hike from Copper Mountain to Frisco.

Looking east from Copper Mountain, the summits of Peak 4, 12,866 feet, and Peak 3, 12,676 feet, in the Tenmile Range form ragged cliffs above Tenmile Creek. Two avalanche chutes drop to form a "U" where the Wheeler National Recreation Trail begins. One mile south of the trailhead, three other avalanche chutes form the letters "SKI" above the Corn Parking Lot along the east side of Highway 91. The Wheeler Trail turns uphill near the base of the "S" chute. The trail continues steadily south without a switchback for 3.6 miles from the trailhead.

In order to access the Wheeler Trail, drive to the trailhead parking area along the frontage road on the south side of I-70, past Copper Mountain Consolidated Metropolitan District Wastewater Reclamation Facility. The Wheeler Trail parking area is beside the Tenmile Creek, 39°30.552' N, 106°08.536' W, at an elevation of 9,690 feet.

From the parking area, hike across two bridges. Turn right to follow Tenmile Creek upstream, one mile south along Highway 91. The trail proceeds to a wooden stock bridge crossing Tenmile Creek that was built fifty years ago.

The junction marks the start of the ascent along the Wheeler Trail, 39°29.640' N, 106°08.137' W, at 9,770 feet. Two hours from the trailhead, 39°28.540' N, 106°06.925' W, at 11,215 feet, the Wheeler Trail meets Miners Creek Trail near tree line below Peak 7, 12,655 feet, and Peak 8, 12,987 feet.

In order to reach Frisco, hike north along the switchback to cross over the Tenmile Range between Peak 5 and Peak 6 on Miners Creek Trail. The Miners Creek Trail reaches the summit pass at 12,530 feet, with a total ascent of about 3,000 feet. The crest of the Tenmile Range is 6.2 miles from the trailhead, N 39 30 279, W 106 06 839.

Six hours into the hike, the Upper Miners Creek Trailhead, 39°31.981' N, 106°05.834' W, is at 10,665 feet. Continue east, crossing Miners Creek again. The trail hooks south briefly around a ridge before crossing another branch of Miners Creek, passing the ruins of miners cabins, and following the creek to a junction with the Peaks Trail. Turn left at the junction with the Peaks Trail, 39°32.015' N, 106°04.845' W, for the final 4 miles down the Miners Creek ravine to Frisco. The trail departs the forest and merges with the Farmers Bike Path and continues north to the entrance to Ophir Mountain Village, 39°34.322' N, 106°05.111' W, beside Highway 9 in Frisco.

The west slope of Peak 8 rises above the junction of the Wheeler Trail and the Miners Creek Trail.

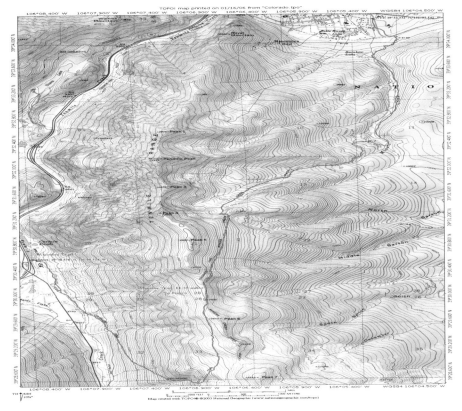

Map created with TOPO! ©2006 National Geographic
http://www.nationalgeographic.com/topo

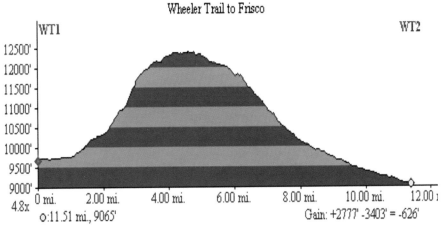

Profile created with TOPO!® ©2003 National Geographic (www.nationalgeographic.com/topo)

Wheeler Trail begins at an elevation of 9,690 feet and ascends to
12,530 feet.

A miner's cabin guards the shore of Lower Crystal Lake.

Lower Crystal Lake Trail

Trailhead   39°25.739' N, 106°04.131' W
Destination   39°26.451' N, 106°05.386' W
Hours   2
Miles   3

Breckenridge was a busy mining area more than a century ago. The Tenmile Range retains scars and remnants of the high elevation mining settlements that once dotted the mountains of Summit County. Mining operations were scattered throughout the steep ravines south of Breckenridge. The remains of one dig lies within the Crystal Creek watershed near Lower Crystal Lake.

The Lower Crystal Lake Trail follows the gradual ascent of an old mining road between Peak 10, 13,633 feet, and Mount Helen, 13,164 feet. During the summer, the path allows easy access to an alpine lake and wildflowers within 2 hours. In winter, the site continues to be accessible for adventurers with snowshoes or cross-country skis, with great views across the Blue River Valley as well as the ragged ridge forming the amphitheater of Crystal Peak, 13,852 feet, and the adjacent summits.

A short drive from Breckenridge, 2.7 miles south of Ski Hill Road on Highway 9, the trail is approached by turning west on Spruce Creek Road, across from Goose Pasture Tarn. The winter trailhead parking area is 1.2 miles up Spruce Creek Road. Crystal Creek Road joins Spruce Creek Road a few tenths of a mile beyond the winter trailhead parking. Crystal Creek Road proceeds west for a mile along Crystal Creek to Francie's Cabin, a bunk-house operated by the Summit Huts Association, near the junction of the Wheeler Trail and Lower Crystal Lake Trail.

Francie's Cabin was constructed in 1994 and named in honor of Frances Lockwood Bailey. The hut can be rented and lodges up to twenty visitors in six small bedrooms at an elevation of 11,264 feet.

When Spruce Creek Road is clear of snow, drive 2.5 miles from the junction with Highway 9 and turn right at the junction with the Wheeler Trail. Turn north and park near the gate on the shoulder of the Forest Service road, 39°25.739' N, 106°04.131' W, at 10,940 feet. Take 80 steps north and turn uphill onto the Wheeler Trail. The trail winds through the forest along the eastern base of Mount Helen. Breaks in the trees along a ridge provide views of Red Mountain, 13,229 feet.

The Wheeler Trail crosses Crystal Creek and joins the Lower Crystal Lake Trail within a half hour hike, N 39 26 256, W 106 04 470, at 11,440 feet. To reach Lower Crystal Lake, turn left, climbing west. Lower Crystal Lake is 1 mile up the old mining road, 39°26.147' N, 106°05.365' W, at 11,970 feet. At the eastern edge of Crystal Lake, a collapsed cabin guards the shoreline. South of the lake, on the face of Mount Helen, is an abandoned mine. For an elevated view of Lower Crystal Lake, continue north 1 mile along the road to the first switchback on Peak 10, 39°26.451' N, 106°05.386' W, at 12,275 feet, and enjoy views of Boreas Pass to the east.

The Wheeler Trail rises to a junction with the Lower Crystal Lake Trail.

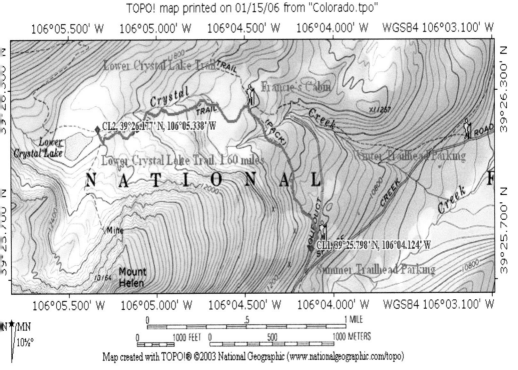

Map created with TOPO! ©2006 National Geographic
http://www.nationalgeographic.com/topo

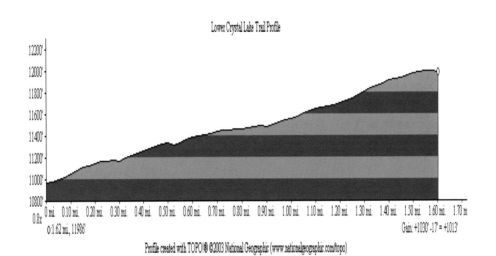

Lower Crystal Lake Trail begins at an elevation of 10,940 feet and
ascends to 11,970 feet.

Fenskes Cranium, balances at12,400 feet on Fletcher Mountain.

Mayflower Gulch Trail

Trailhead   39°25.822' N, 106°09.914' W
Destination   39°24.399' N, 106°08.962' W
Hours   4
Miles   6

Whether searching for a short hike with a gentle ascent through mining ruins or a backcountry adventure to a telemark run into a deep powder bowl above the trees, Mayflower Gulch fills the order. Situated on the quiet western slope of the Tenmile Range near Leadville, Mayflower Gulch is a haven for wildflowers in summer and crests of deep snow crowning lonely cabin debris through the long Summit County winter.

From I-70 west of Frisco, Mayflower Gulch is 5.8 miles south of the Copper Mountain Village entrance on Highway 91. A trailhead parking area, 39°25.822' N, 106°09.914' W, is situated across from the first tailings pond at the Climax Mine industrial area, at the lofty elevation of 10,935 feet. Across the highway is the plain once occupied by the Town of Kokomo, with a booming population of 1,500 in 1879, the first year it was established.

Ascend east from the trailhead along an old mining access road for 1.8 miles to the site of exploratory diggings of the Boston Mining Company, 39°24.762' N, 106°08.809' W, at an elevation of 11,580 feet. Along the way, a cabin rests along the north shoulder of the road, with the remains of an ore chute on the south side of the road.

Explore the Boston Mine buildings across Mayflower Creek. Continue to the mining shack near the base of the dramatic amphitheater created by Crystal Mountain, 13,951 feet. From the north, Pacific Creek slices through a dramatic ravine from Pacific Peak, 13,950 feet, to join Mayflower Creek.

The ridge of Gold Hill, at 12,060 feet, is 2.6 miles from the trailhead, about 1,000 feet above Clinton Reservoir which stretches west along the southern face of Gold Hill. Looking northwest along the ridge of Gold Hill, Jacque Peak, 13,205, rises sharply beyond Tenmile Creek. The climb to this point, 39°24.605' N, 106°09.108' W, is approximately 2 hours and provides access to powder stashes for the backcountry skier in winter.

From the end of the mining road, ascend east along the ridge to the first promontory of curvaceous Fletcher Mountain, 3 miles from the trailhead. A rounded rock at 12,370 feet, precariously balanced over the edge, 39°24.399' N, 106°08.962' W, is dubbed Fenskes Cranium for its hard-headed stubbornness.

While the final ascent of the hike is arduous and risky, the view of snow blowing over the sharp chess pieces on Bartlett Mountain to the south, down into the Clinton Amphitheater, steals the breath. As sunset gold covers the mountains of the Holy Cross Wilderness Area along the Continental Divide, the speculations of busted miners sparkling in their eyes more than a century ago can easily be understood and laid to rest.

The amphitheater of Fletcher Mountain overlooks Mayflower Gulch.

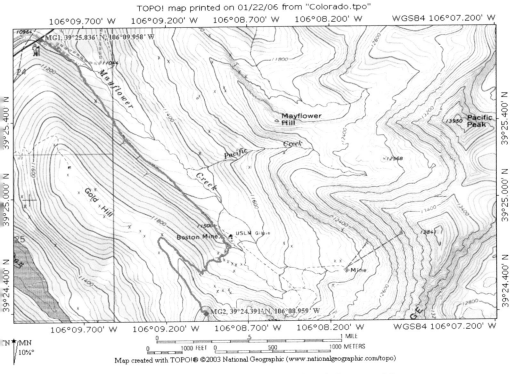

Map created with TOPO! ©2006 National Geographic
http://www.nationalgeographic.com/topo

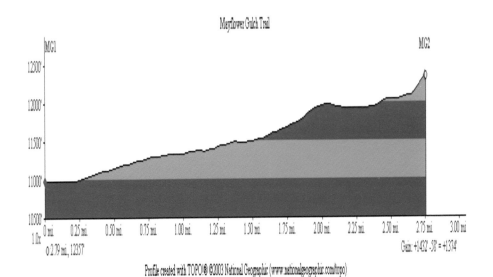

Mayflower Gulch Trail begins at an elevation of 10,935 feet and ascends to 12,400 feet.

Jacque Peak, 13,205 feet, stands west of mining ruins at Clinton Gulch.

Clinton Gulch Reservoir Trail

Trailhead	39°24.943' N, 106°10.280' W
Destination	39°24.144' N, 106°08.642' W
Hours	3
Miles	5

Looking south from the summit of Copper Mountain, the craggy, wind-swept peak of Bartlett Mountain, looms in the distance above Clinton Creek. Capturing the flow of melting snow before it joins Tenmile Creek is the dam of Clinton Gulch Reservoir. In summer, Clinton Reservoir is a great place to catch cutthroat trout. In winter, the slopes of Gold Hill and Carbonate Hill are a white wonderland with diminishing marks of forgotten mining ventures jutting from the drifts of snow.

A hike of 5 hours, Clinton Gulch Reservoir Trail begins at a parking pad on the north side of Clinton Reservoir. From the junction of Interstate 70 and Highway 91, drive 7 miles south of the entrance to Copper Mountain Village. Turn left into the parking area, 39° 24.943' N, 106°10.280' W, and hike east to a junction with an old mining road. The trailhead is at an elevation of 11,200 feet, giving this hike an ascent of about 1,200 feet.

To the right of Clinton Reservoir is Bartlett Mountain, 13,555 feet, with Wheeler Mountain, 13,690 feet, at the rear of Clinton Gulch. Beyond the ridge to the east are Blue Lakes at the base of Quandary Peak, 14,265 feet.

Follow the mining road, ascending north to the spine of Gold Hill. Along the way, enjoy viewing Jacque Peak, 13,205, and Elk Mountain, 12,095, across the Climax Mine tailings ponds at the site of the long lost mining town of Kokomo. Mining cabin ruins and foundation holes are scattered among the lodge pole pines that remain on the cut-over slopes of Gold Hill.

The top of Gold Hill, 12,060 feet, is an open tree-less expanse that provides great views of the surrounding mountains. In the west, the watershed of the East Fork Eagle River forms the edge of Eagle County. Chicago Ridge, 12,542 feet, is in the distance, south of Camp Hale. In the north, Union Mountain, 12,313 feet, and Copper Mountain 12,441, create a foreground for the distant Gore Range.

Continuing east, more patches of past mining ventures cover the summit of Gold Hill. Within 2 hours, about 3 miles from the trailhead, the base of Fletcher Mountain rises abruptly in a tumbled array of boulders. Fenskes Cranium, a precariously-balanced rock overlooking Mayflower Gulch to the north, marks 12,400 feet before a steep scramble to the first summit along the knife-edge amphitheater of Fletcher Mountain. Climb as high as daring allows, then descend and explore the shoreline of the Clinton Gulch Reservoir. Please carry a bag along to fill with bottles and other debris that may be found near the parking area.

Clinton Reservoir glistens at the base of Bartlett Mountain.

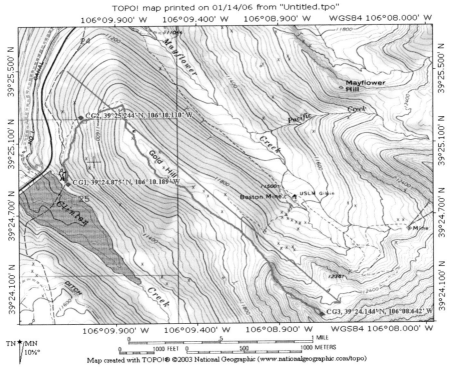

Map created with TOPO! ©2006 National Geographic
http://www.nationalgeographic.com/topo

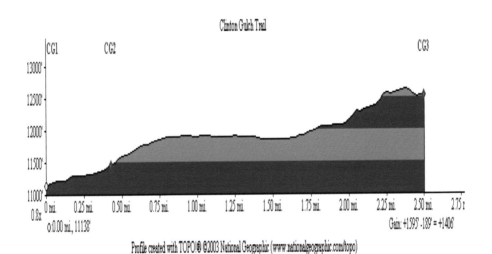

Clinton Gulch Trail begins at an elevation of 11,200 feet and
ascends to 12,400 feet.

Mayflower Lake hides the ruins of many early settlement cabins.

Spruce Creek Trail

Trailhead	39°25.273' N, 106°04.434' W
Destination	39°25.153' N, 106°05.407' W
Hours	2
Miles	3

The Spruce Creek Trail offers direct contact with mining camp ruins from more than a century ago. The area also provides access to the intimate Mayflower Lakes, satin sheets of Continental Falls, Lower Mohawk Lake, and Mohawk Lake, with views of Mount Helen, Crystal Peak, and Pacific Peak.

Spruce Creek watershed lies two miles south of Breckenridge in the Tenmile Range near the Town of Blue River. Driving south of Breckenridge along Highway 9, turn right across from Goose Pasture Tarn, one-half mile past Crown Drive. Follow Spruce Creek Road to the west for a little more than a mile to the winter parking area at the portal of the White River Forest. Spruce Creek Trailhead is north of the parking area. In summer, a high-clearance vehicle can continue nearly two miles up the Forest Service road to the trailhead at McCullough Tunnel, 39°25.273' N, 106°04.434' W, part of the Blue River Diversion Project.

During winter, one hour of a gentle climb west from the trailhead, at about 10,200 feet, leads to the intersection with the Wheeler National Recreation Trail at 11,000 feet. The Wheeler Trail crosses the Ten Mile Range to the northwest and drops into Copper Mountain and also continues south from Spruce Creek to the Continental Divide at Hoosier Pass.

Another hour of climbing, slightly more than a mile of hiking, passes McCullough Tunnel and opens the forest to one of the Mayflower Lakes, at 11,300 feet. The ruins of a log cabin remain south of the lake at the edge of Spruce Creek. Overhead, search the cliff to the west for the tower of an ore conveyance that remains at approximately 11,800 feet. In winter, drifts of deep powder deter penetration beyond the Mayflower Lakes. During the summer, a stream crossing leads to switchbacks up the next thousand feet of elevation beside Continental Falls to Lower Mohawk Lake.

Lower Mohawk Lake is nestled against the southern base of Mount Helen, 13,164 feet. Spruce Creek descends swiftly from several lakes below Pacific Peak, 13,950, at the west end of the ravine. Crystal Peak, 13,852 feet, and Father Dyer Peak, 13, 615 feet, stand guard in the north. From Lower Mohawk Lake a trail ascends south to Mohawk Lake, 39°25.153' N, 106°05.407' W, at an elevation of 12,200 feet, two thousand feet above the trailhead.

Beginning with a major gold rush in 1859, miners undoubtedly appreciated Spruce Creek as a source of panning gravel. However, modern explorers may respect the watershed as a place of natural splendor with gnarly willow bogs, ancient spruce, dense lodgepole pine, and clinging columbine standing watch over the ravine. Spruce Creek steadily tumbles to the Blue River, a horizon of Red Mountain and Boreas Pass at the Continental Divide in the east. Spruce Creek remains an area of scenic treasure despite being stripped of precious metals more than a dozen decades ago.

Evidence of mining operations still exists near Lower Mohawk Lake.

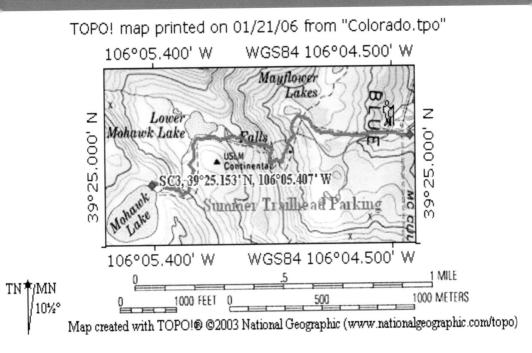

Map created with TOPO! ©2006 National Geographic
http://www.nationalgeographic.com/topo

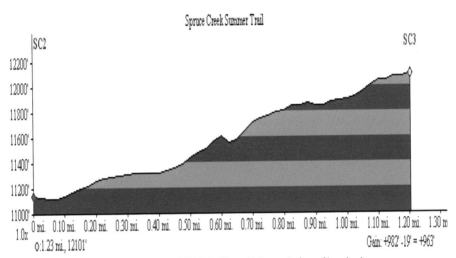

Spruce Creek Trail begins at an elevation of 10,200 feet and
ascends to 12,200 feet.

Quandary Peak overlooks Fletcher Peak and the rugged peaks beyond.

Quandary Peak

Trailhead	39°23.124' N, 106°03.723' W
Destination	39°23.857' N, 106°06.390' W
Hours	4
Miles	6

One of the great assets of Summit County is access to high terrain rising above tree-line to offer spectacular views of many miles of surrounding mountain peaks. Quandary Peak, with an altitude of 14,249 feet, provides relatively easy access to the great heights characteristic of Colorado. Situated at the southernmost end of Summit County, Quandary Peak rises a thousand feet above the summits of the Tenmile and Gore Range to the north, allowing hikers to see mountains a hundred miles away on a clear day. Sunset from Quandary Peak is an explosion of colors covering a vast area of sky from the plains beyond Hoosier Pass in the south to the Ptarmigan Wilderness Area in the north.

The Quandary Peak summit is attained in one hour of ascent along a forested trail and a few more hours up a ridge of wind-exposed rock field above tree-line. The climb is about three miles, starting at an altitude of 11,120 feet and ending at the summit three thousand feet higher.

The trailhead for the Quandary Peak Trail is approximately eight miles south of Breckenridge along Colorado State Highway 9, beyond the Town of Blue River. After taking the first switchback of Hoosier Pass, turn right onto Blue Lakes Road and, for winter access, park at the intersection with Mc-Cullough Gulch Road immediately to the right. Trailhead interpretive displays are a hundred feet north along McCullough Gulch Road, 39°23.124' N, 106°03.723' W, with the trail winding west through the trees to the left. The trail remains a clearly marked pathway, rising among old mining ventures in a lodgepole pine and spruce forest. Near tree-line, glimpses of the summit appear from openings in the trees.

As it leaves the forest and passes clumps of short willows, the trail intersects with a former access route from the south that has been restored and re-vegetated with the efforts of volunteers under the direction of the Forest Service and Colorado Fourteeners Initiative. Above deep drifts of blown snow at this junction, exposed talus fields provide clear ascent along a ridge to the summit, 39°23.857' N, 106°06.390' W.

Across the frozen Blue Lakes formed by blocking the flow of Monte Cristo Creek to the south, North Star Mountain provides a rugged ridgeline with mining ruins along its steep face. Beyond North Star and the Continental Divide, lies Mount Lincoln, 14,286 feet in height, within Park County. Rising above the trees to the east is Red Mountain, with the twin fourteeners, Grays and Torreys, in the northeast. At the summit, the Mount of the Holy Cross can be observed to the west, with the Tenmile Range melding with the Gore Range to the north.

Immediately north of Quandary Peak is the drainage of McCullough Gulch Creek, providing clusters of columbine clinging to the rock walls in summer and whirlpool grottos carved over millenia sheltering intimate waterfalls below active mining claims. East of Pacific Peak, 13,950, Spruce Creek flows down the rocky ravine, with a hiking trail passing Mayflower Falls and abandoned mining cabins throughout its watershed.

The Quandary Peak Trail follows a ridge west to the mountain summit.

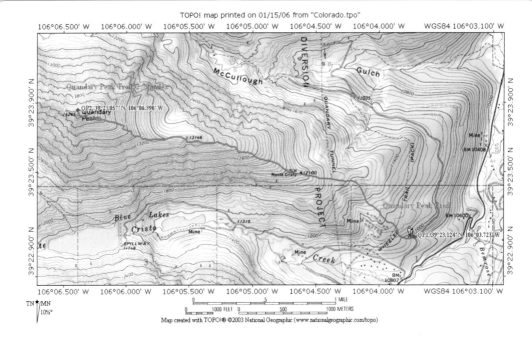

Map created with TOPO! ©2006 National Geographic
http://www.nationalgeographic.com/topo

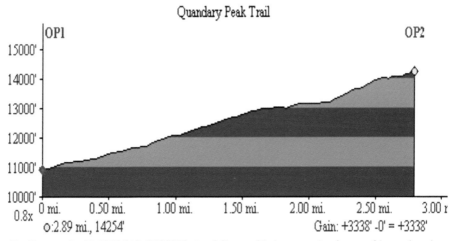

Profile created with TOPO!® ©2003 National Geographic (www.nationalgeographic.com/topo)

Quandary Peak Trail begins at an elevation of 11,120 feet and
ascends to 14,265 feet.

Index of Wildflowers

The Author

Kim Fenske explores the wilderness trails of Central Colorado, identifying and photographing wildlife, building and maintaining pathways, and guiding visitors to adventures on public lands. In Summit County, he is the Backcountry Report columnist and photographer for the *County Cable*. He has years of service on the executive boards of Friends of the Eagles Nest Wilderness Area and Sierra Club.

As an attorney, the author served in low-income housing development and environmental regulation. His background includes more than a decade of teaching, with an emphasis on issues affecting the environment.

He served on the staff of the Wisconsin State Assembly Environmental Resources Committee, reviewed environmental issues with the Department of Justice Public Intervenors Office, and ran for the Wisconsin State Assembly.

Acknowledgments

The author thanks his mother, Norma Johnson Fenske, who allowed him to run free in the woods. When needed, she provided him with food and shelter. He recognizes his father, Arthur Fenske, for giving him an appreciation for national parks, forests, and wilderness areas. In addition, the author thanks his sisters Sally Fenske Rix and Julie Fenske Christensen for providing the resources necessary to complete this work during seasons of unemployment.

Furthermore, the author thanks botanist Nancy Redner for technical assistance with the identification of Colorado wildflowers. He also remembers the inspiration of his uncle, botanist Allan Johnson, artistic encouragement from his aunt, Alice Fenske Solik, and understanding by teachers throughout his years of creative development.